BECOMING
NORMAL

AN
EVER-CHANGING
PERSPECTIVE

CENTRAL RECOVERY PRESS

CENTRAL RECOVERY PRESS

Central Recovery Press (CRP) is committed to publishing exceptional
material addressing addiction treatment, recovery, and behavioral health
care, including original and quality books, audio/visual communications,
and web-based new media. Through a diverse selection of titles, it seeks
to impact the behavioral health care field with a broad range of unique
resources for professionals, recovering individuals, and their families. For
more information, visit www.centralrecoverypress.com.

Central Recovery Press, Las Vegas, NV 89129
© 2010 by Utopia Bookworks, Inc.

ISBN-13: 978-0-9818482-1-1
ISBN-10: 0-9818482-1-4

16 15 14 13 12 11 10   1 2 3 4 5

Publisher: Central Recovery Press
            3371 N Buffalo Drive
            Las Vegas, NV 89129

Cover design and interior by Sara Streifel, Think Creative Design

To the most patient, loving
person I know: my mother.

To the rest of my family,
who never gave up on me.

To my first sponsor and his wife,
who helped me find my way from
the dark into the light.

AS I PRACTICE I BECOME MORE PROFICIENT, AND AS I BECOME MORE PROFICIENT THE PRACTICE BECOMES MORE SECOND-NATURE, UNTIL ONE DAY I REALIZE THAT PRACTICING THE PRINCIPLES IS A NORMAL PART OF THE WAY I CONDUCT MYSELF.

I AM "BECOMING NORMAL."

CONTENTS

I MUST ALLOW FOR MISTAKES.

MISTAKES ARE NORMAL.

ACKNOWLEDGMENTS

I would like to thank my editors, Daniel Kaelin and Helen O'Reilly, for their tireless work in the editing process. Their incalculable effort made this project possible.

I would also like to thank Mary Fouty at Lansing Community College (LCC), who helped me with the original manuscript. I think she still wonders if offering her help was a good idea, but I'll never forget how beneficial her input was during those early days.

Jill Pennington, who runs the Writing Center at LCC, taught me that writing is a process I need to enjoy, which led me to discover that life is a process I also need to enjoy.

Leslie Farris, another writing instructor, taught me not to argue without giving the other person credit for their point of view. I do my best, Leslie.

Thanks also to all my other writing instructors who have helped me practice the process of writing, learning, and life.

I want to thank Central Recovery Press for providing the pages and ink that make up this book. They have done more than that: They took a chance on me, for which I will be forever grateful.

I also want to thank you, my reading friend; I hope that you will find my thanks expressed in the experiences and learning I have shared in these pages.

Lastly, but most importantly, I want to thank God. Without His help, none of this would have happened.

IN EVERY AREA OF MY LIFE, I CAN MAKE REMARKABLE PROGRESS. THROUGH THIS PROGRESS, I COME CLOSER TO NORMAL— WHATEVER THAT IS, ANYWAY!

HOW I STOPPED WORRYING AND LEARNED TO BECOME NORMAL OR PRACTICING THE PRINCIPLES

I've spent way too much of my life worrying about whether or not I was normal, and maybe you have, too—especially if your life has been affected by your addiction or that of another, such as a sibling, parent, child, or spouse. "Am I okay?" "Do I fit in?" "What will others think?" and ultimately, "Is there something wrong with me?" are questions that plagued me my entire life, causing me excessive concern about whether or not I was, in fact, normal.

My disease of addiction only made me feel more abnormal, more apart from my fellow men and women. Recovery through my twelve-step fellowship finally allowed me to stop worrying about normalcy and appreciate myself for the person my Higher Power wants me to be, the person I know I am becoming as I journey through my recovery adventure.

My journey to understanding the meaning of "normal" took many twists and turns, and involved me in intricate strategies I devised for myself, even after I entered recovery. But ultimately, my relief, and my understanding of what normal means for me, came through working the Twelve Steps of my program of recovery.

What follows is my story.

PRACTICING THE PRINCIPLES

NOTE: *Many spiritual principles are associated with the Twelve Steps of recovery. These principles overlap and repeat throughout the steps. No one step calls for only one principle, and the principles listed here are by no means the only ones associated with the steps under discussion; however, they are the ones that I discovered and developed in myself by working each particular step.*

STEP ONE. THE PRINCIPLE: ACCEPTANCE

When I first came to my fellowship, I was powerless over my addiction; I still am. Does this mean I'm not normal? Absolutely not. As long as I accept that I do not and cannot pick up, I can live quite normally.

Very early in my recovery I was told that Step One was the only step I had to get one hundred percent right— and I believed it! I cannot drink, drug, or engage in other manifestations of addiction and properly practice the remaining steps (or do much of anything else).

Through the principle of acceptance, I now realize the truth of the matter. I am okay with the reality of my condition. I am an imperfect human being, just like everybody else, and yet I am just as normal as anyone else.

STEP TWO. THE PRINCIPLE: FAITH

When I came to believe that a Power greater than myself could restore me to physical, mental, spiritual, and emotional health, this step began to work for me.

With the second step, I learned to right-size. I discovered I was not the center of the universe. I was not the be-all-and-end-all; I could not even solve my own problems. More of me was never enough when dealing with life. I needed something more than myself. I soon discovered that in order to find something greater, I had to become smaller! I had to join the rest of those on the planet, by being more human.

Through faith I was able to leap from my self-constructed pedestal. The key was faith in the idea that those who had gone before me might actually know what they were talking about. It was faith—with a little hope thrown in—that allowed me to try something new, to go in a different direction, and to open my mind to strange new ideas, which made me uncomfortable for a time. In the process, I learned that I *was* normal after all; I have the same capabilities as other people. I only need to learn to use them properly.

STEP THREE. THE PRINCIPLES: SURRENDER AND TRUST

When I consciously decided to turn both my will and my life over to the care of a God of my understanding (or Higher Power), I learned that by replacing reliance on my own abilities with reliance on God, as I understood God, I could accomplish things I might never have dreamed possible. By doing my best to surrender and trust, by turning my will and my life over to the will of God each day, I free myself from the bondage of working for results.

Through surrender and trust, I've learned to be more relaxed about what happens in my life. I can do my share and leave the results up to God. (I happen to believe this is about as normal as I can possibly be.) When I am in the groove of God's will, I feel better than I ever thought I would. After all, God's will is going to happen with or without me. I can choose to go along with it, or I can fight it. However, if I choose to fight, I am wasting valuable time and energy.

STEP FOUR. THE PRINCIPLE: HONESTY

When I finally looked at my past life fearlessly and thoroughly, making the moral inventory of myself that Step Four demands, I realized that I had spent all of my todays being haunted by my yesterdays. Writing a list of all my resentments, fears, and missteps in life was not an easy chore, but in doing it I was able to put down the burden of self that I had been carrying with me all day, every day. That's a lot of baggage to cart around all the time. Writing down my inventory was the crucial step toward ridding myself of my past's garbage, which was so necessary as I strove toward becoming normal. Today I can be honest, because I've learned to be honest with myself first of all. In order to be honest with others, I must become completely, totally, and rigorously honest with myself.

STEP FIVE. THE PRINCIPLE: COURAGE

When I summoned the courage to admit to God, to myself, and to another human being the exact nature of my wrongs, I finally rid myself of the baggage of my past. This took tremendous courage. I thought doing so would leave me empty. I thought I would become a cipher, a nothing. Even though my past was garbage, for the most part I wanted to cling to it because it was all I knew. I was afraid of sharing all my most negative actions with another person; I was also afraid to give myself to the unknown.

I still do not know what happened, but I never did lose myself. My past was still intact; it just did not wield the force it once had. Just as *I* had become right-sized in the previous steps, my past became more right-sized when I completed Step Five. I came to see my past for what it was—my past. It is what made me who I am today, but it is not *who* I am today. While I am a product of my past, I am not simply a compilation of my past acts and experiences. "I am greater than the sum of my parts." While I have done some bad things—made some bad choices—I can now begin to learn from them. Perhaps you can learn from yours, too.

This step calls for courage, and completing it actually builds courage. The courage I gained from doing this step is a bonus, in that it helped me to move forward and to pass through walls of fear I would most likely have avoided without this crucial step.

STEP SIX. THE PRINCIPLE: WILLINGNESS

When I was completely ready to have God take away the character defects that had been uncovered by the fifth step, and I finally became willing to let God have a go at them, I learned the value of asking for help.

I do not know if asking for help is normal or not, but I do know it makes life a whole lot easier. Today I ask for help, and that is normal for me, although it was never normal for me to ask before, no matter how much I thought I needed it.

STEP SEVEN. THE PRINCIPLE: HUMILITY

When I asked my Higher Power, humbly, to remove my shortcomings, I began to see myself for who and what I really am. I am a fallible human being doing my best with the tools I have. The bonus is that I can also see other people for who and what they are—fallible human beings doing the best they can with the tools they have, human beings who are neither more nor less normal than I am. I lose being judgmental of myself and others and I can operate more freely, while allowing others to do the same. Humility helps me see just how normal I really am.

STEP EIGHT. THE PRINCIPLE: FORGIVENESS

When I made a list of all the persons my past actions had harmed and became willing to make amends to them, I began to experience forgiveness, including forgiveness of myself. This went a long way toward reassuring me that I was indeed normal, although I never would have believed it in the old days.

STEP NINE. THE PRINCIPLE: FREEDOM

When I began to make amends to the people on my eighth-step list, it seemed like the most unnatural thing I could possibly do. Although I still find making amends difficult, I do so when necessary because the results bring me back to a more normal state, and, of course, because it is required for my recovery. Sometimes I have to get my hands dirty, so to speak, in order to maintain my sense of normalcy, but it is always worth the effort.

After making amends to all those on my Step Nine list, I discovered, through Step Ten, that I had made an error in judgment and inadvertently wronged someone. I did not even know the person I had wronged very well, but I became very nervous around the person whenever we happened to be in the same room or area. When I knew he was near, I was a nervous wreck. The gaffe was entirely my fault, and I was pretty sure he would not forgive me. Still, I knew I had to rid myself of the guilt in order to continue in my own recovery. I also knew, from working my way through Step Nine, that this experience is really all about cleaning my side of the street—I am not to concern myself with being forgiven. I make amends in order to find freedom.

Cleaning away the debris of my mistakes gives me freedom to grow. By swallowing my pride, then doing what I have learned to be right, proper, and normal, I free myself from the bondage of my errors. So I made my amends with the person I had wronged. Surprisingly—at least to me—he forgave me. Even if he had not, I knew I had done my best to correct the situation, I was truly sorry, and I would do everything in my power to make sure I do not make the same mistake again. When I see this person today, I do not get nervous. We speak politely, we debate issues, and we get along. I am free to grow and he knows that I know I was wrong and that I will do my best not to let it happen again. When I make amends to others, everybody wins.

Even though making amends can be difficult, the results bring me back—or, sometimes, move me forward—to a state of normalcy. I feel more at ease and better equipped to live my life without worry over things that might happen because I did not clean up my messes.

One of the wonderful lessons I have learned from doing my ninth step is to be more careful about how I behave, so I do not have to make more amends than necessary. Thanks to this step, I have not only freed myself from the baggage of my past, but I have learned valuable lessons about how to conduct myself in the present.

One of the best ways I make my amends these days is to discontinue engaging in my addiction. This is an ongoing amend, and a change I have committed to. Through following this path of ongoing amends I live a more normal life—a life that is becoming more normal to me all the time.

STEP TEN. THE PRINCIPLE: PERSEVERANCE

When I continued to take personal inventory and promptly admitted my wrongdoings (when I realized I had committed them), my life came into greater order. When I persevere in practicing the tenth step, I look at what I have done to ensure I am acting properly—or normally.

Since I discovered the advantages of this step, I have been putting it to use in an ever-more-expedient manner all the time. This step has allowed me, on many occasions, to avoid making mistakes. I am learning to keep my mouth shut when it could do more harm than good to open it. I am learning to consider other people's feelings before taking any action, and I am learning how my actions might affect others in general.

After practicing the tenth step for a short time, I began to see how it was helping me act more normally. I was causing less turmoil in my life and in the lives of those around me.

STEP ELEVEN. THE PRINCIPLE: PATIENCE

When I first sought to improve my conscious contact with God, as I understood God, patience was near the bottom of my list of assets. I wanted tomorrow's results yesterday, and sometimes that was not fast enough. Seeking to improve my conscious contact with God has helped me greatly in this area, because, as I have learned, God does things in His time, not mine. Since He is the One responsible for the results, I had to wait, whether I liked it or not. This was a new concept to me. Acceptance helped me with this new concept, but it still was not easy in the beginning. I began to pray every day, morning and night, from my very first day of recovery. Some days I had to be patient with myself because I could not slow my mind down enough even to pray. I had to take time to really focus in order to get the job done. Learning to be patient with myself helped me be more patient with others. Prayer reminds me of who is really in charge of the results. It is not me; it is not any other person, either. It is God.

When I remember who is in charge, I can slow down, and I can be more patient with myself and others. I can let God do His part. Through this process, I can be more calm, relaxed, and serene. This, in turn, helps me to act more normally. After all, when I am calm and relaxed I can think straight. When I am angry and all keyed up, I do not think very well, if at all, before I act. When I think first, I act more properly and more normally.

Daily prayer keeps me focused on what is important.

Prayer keeps me closer to God as I understand Him today, so when He guides me I can move on with full faith that I will be growing better and faster than before, that I will "bear more fruit," so to speak, instead of feeling a need to know "why me?" in cases where "bad" things happen. If I can apply some patience—allow God to care for me—I will always find a benefit; I will always find growth, which, again, is normal.

STEP TWELVE. THE PRINCIPLES: CHARITY AND LOVE

As the spiritual awakening promised in this step took hold, and I did as the step suggests, I began to carry the recovery message to others, and began to practice the principles of all the steps in everything I did.

It's hard to decide whether this is the most difficult step or the easiest. I know now that a spiritual awakening will happen of its own accord, if I work the steps. My job is to work the steps, and let God do His job, providing a spiritual awakening for me. Therefore, the first part of this step happens normally as I practice the program.

I learn valuable lessons about life. This is especially true when considering charity and love. I learn that through giving I receive. I had to learn this, because I once thought I received through taking. This is a valuable lesson—this lesson of giving. It teaches me to love whether I want to or not, because I almost never get to choose the people I help; they seem to choose me. The people I have sponsored over the years have always asked me to help them—they did the choosing—my part was simply to be of service. I learned to love them, every one of them, and some of the people I have sponsored I most certainly would not have chosen. God provides the people and the love. All I have to do is do my best to do my part.

Once I had tasted charity and love—and saw what they can do—my desire to continue along this path was heightened, and I discovered I wanted more. There is one final purpose to the twelfth step. I have heard it said that practicing the principles of the program in everything we do is the key to the whole program.

If I could put all of the principles into action, I would be a very busy man. Fortunately, the step says I can practice them, and practice implies that I will make mistakes along the way. In fact, the mistakes themselves help me practice the principles. I must become honest enough to admit the mistakes, while perseverance helps me move forward with the rest of what needs doing. Acceptance keeps me from beating myself up too badly about making a mistake, while patience keeps me from trying to just patch things over if they need a total rebuild. Faith helps me know things will work out if I surrender the outcome to God and trust that He will take care of things. When I find humility, I become willing to forgive wherever necessary, including forgiving myself, and then I summon the courage to make amends, which provides the freedom to move back to charity and love. Of course, it does not always happen in this order, or with this kind of ease. However, as I practice I become more proficient, and as I become more proficient the practice becomes more second-nature, until one day I realize that practicing the principles is a normal part of the way I conduct myself. I am "becoming normal."

THIS WENT A LONG WAY TOWARD REASSURING ME THAT I WAS INDEED NORMAL, ALTHOUGH I NEVER WOULD HAVE BELIEVED IT IN THE OLD DAYS.

IF I TOLD MYSELF THAT NO

MATTER HOW MUCH I GROW I

WILL NEVER BECOME NORMAL,

I WOULD SIMPLY ADD TO THIS

DESIRE TO BECOME NORMAL

A MEASURE OF FEAR THAT

SAYS IF I SHOULD SOMEHOW

REACH THAT PEDESTAL I

WOULD MOST CERTAINLY

FALL OFF, OR AT LEAST BE

IN DANGER OF DOING SO.

1

WHAT IS NORMAL, ANYWAY?

For me, normal once meant drinking and drugging. Mood- and mind-altering substances, including alcohol, brought me to my knees. My addiction had many manifestations, but a single common thread. Its power lay in what I thought of myself, what I thought others thought of me, and my reaction to what I was thinking. This is my story—how I went from being a drunk to being someone who chooses not to drink. My story is about my old idea of normal and how, through recovery, I was able to define and re-create my new understanding of what I believe normal is.

In recovery, I discovered how my thinking perpetuated my drinking and how my thoughts and my addiction shaped my life. Through the process of working the Twelve Steps in my recovery fellowship, I was able to completely change my relationship with my addiction, and I came to understand why I viewed those who could drink or use socially or recreationally in such a different way. With the help of my sponsor, other members of my fellowship, my twelve-step work, and my Higher Power, I have been able to transform my life in ways I never thought possible. Self-acceptance allowed me to discover that I already was normal. I just did not know how normal I really was.

When I first heard people in my recovery fellowship talk about normal people, or "normies," as some call them, I used to wince. It was as if normal people and people in recovery were two distinct classes of human being—different from each other, distant from each other, and therefore, unable to understand each other. But as I searched for a greater understanding of what it means to be normal, I learned to get along with all kinds of people, in and out of recovery, for the sake of my own personal growth.

I learned that I limit my growth by the way I define normal. Some I met early in recovery seemed to me to view so-called "normal people" as though they were greater or better than themselves. It seemed to me that some people I met in early recovery thought that those who could drink or use socially—nonaddicts, in other words—had some kind of mystical power that elevated them above those who cannot do these things. They had a word for them: "normies." These normies seemed to me to occupy an imaginary pedestal in the minds of others in recovery. They certainly occupied a special place in *my* thinking early on. But I came to realize that if I put these people on a higher plane than my fellows in recovery, I'd place serious limitations on how far I could grow. If I told myself that no matter how much I grow I will never become normal, I would simply add to this desire to become normal a measure of fear that says if I should somehow reach that pedestal I would most certainly fall off, or at least be in danger of doing so. Over time I have learned to discard these thoughts and feelings, because they are self-defeating.

This understanding helps me to see that my program allows me to live life without destroying myself with mind- and mood-altering substances. This gives me a shot at becoming normal (whatever that is). I am neither better nor worse than any other person; I am equal to others. This newfound equality gives me the freedom to grow and to reach my full potential. By removing these self-imposed limits, caused by my distorted thinking about myself and about others, I gain the ability to become so much more than I am today. In every area of my life, I can make remarkable progress. Through this progress, I come closer to normal—whatever that is, anyway!

Recovery helped me to redefine my understanding of normal.

IT SEEMS THAT LIKE MOST

PEOPLE, I HAVE A BUILT-IN

NEED TO FEEL THAT I AM PART

OF THE WORLD AND PART OF

SOCIETY. THIS NEED DRIVES

MY DESIRE TO UNDERSTAND

WHAT IT IS TO BE NORMAL

AND HAS PROMPTED ME TO

SPEND TIME LEARNING HOW

TO FIT INTO SOCIETY.

2

FITTING IN— IS THAT WHAT IT MEANS TO BE NORMAL?

I have heard many people in recovery say that they never felt like they fit in anywhere. They always felt different from the people with whom they grew up. This is a common sentiment among members of recovery groups. For the most part, I could identify. I had few friends, and the ones I did have always seemed to be getting into trouble of some kind, and I was right there with them: lying, stealing, cheating, and carousing. These things were all part of life as far as we were concerned. These feelings set us apart from the majority, we thought. We were selfish and self-centered, and sought instant gratification. My friends and I thought we were tough and cool, but in reality we were nothing more than public nuisances, disturbing the peace and doing whatever we felt like, whenever we felt like it, without regard for anyone else's property or peace of mind. Acting in this way alienated others, who found our actions irritating, annoying, and even crazy. It is no wonder I felt as though I did not fit in, so after a while I did not even try. If you'd asked me then, I would have denied it, but today I know that fitting in was exactly what I wanted.

The truth is that I have always wanted to fit in, and today I do, because I am in recovery. It seems that like most people, I have a built-in need to feel that I am part of the world and part of society. This need drives my desire to understand what it is to be normal and has prompted me to spend time learning how to fit into society. Today, I am learning to smooth off my rough spots so I can fit better into life as it is really is, not as I'd like it to be. In order to do this, obviously, I had to quit drinking, but that was only one step. I had previously, and more easily, set aside marijuana and cocaine. However, for me, quitting drinking was the most important step toward a new way of life. This manifestation of my addiction was my greatest challenge, and I needed to meet it head-on and with all the courage I could summon.

One of the reasons quitting drinking and drugging was so difficult for me was that in the beginning, using *had* helped me to feel as though I fit in, as it does for so many others. The illusion or delusion of fitting in while I was drunk was a tough one to break. I did not have any desire to break away from the thought or the substance until it became clear that the reason I gave myself for using was not, in fact, true. Only after it became painfully clear, through time spent in jail and the insistence of friends and family members, that I had a problem, as well as the realization that my using really wasn't helping me fit in anymore, was I able to begin to change.

Once I decided to make the change from active addict to person in recovery, my desire to become normal seemed to grow. I had never liked feeling like an outsider, but now I felt like more of one! While I was using, I had *seemed* to fit in with the other addicts, but I had never tried fitting in while in recovery. Still, I wanted to fit in more than ever.

What does "fitting in" mean, and why was it so important to me? To "fit in" means to me that I will be more loved, more cared for, and more needed. I longed for these feelings. I yearned for these feelings. I spent my entire life seeking real love, true caring, and a greater feeling of being needed. Yet I had always come up short. *If only I could be normal,* I thought; *then I would fit in the way I've always wanted to.*

I know I'm not unique in this regard: It seems that we all want to fit in somewhere. But the thing I thought was helping me fit in was having the opposite effect. I spent too much of my life far from normal, getting loaded, acting in ways that even I didn't accept as proper. Once I stopped drinking and using other mood-altering substances, I began to have a shot at becoming normal and fitting in with the rest of society. This idea was so novel, so untried, that at times it seemed impossible. However, I know that it *is* possible, and I'm giving it a shot.

When I arrived in my twelve-step fellowship, I found something I had been yearning for my entire life. I discovered there were many people just like me, and I easily fit in. We understood each other; we spoke the same language. We laughed at the crazy things we used to do and cried over the traumas we had caused. We "got" each other; we knew where each other had been. Why shouldn't we? We had all been through very similar wringers. We shared the same delusions, illusions, hopes, and dreams. What a wonderful feeling to find people I could relate to without being drunk. What a joyous thing to have people who understood me, who shared my feelings, my fears, and my longing to be cared for, to be needed, and to be loved. My fellowship saved my life, and I will be forever grateful. Of course, as we say in my fellowship, "you can't keep it unless you give it away," and that's what I practice now, and hope to for the rest of my life.

One of the great things about my fellowship is the inclusiveness. As I see it, my fellowship keeps the doors open to a wide range of thinking and ways of dealing with problems. In fact, the door is always open and anyone can get in. To join, all I needed was a problem and a desire to stop. The first thing my fellowship and program did for me was to help me stop. The second thing the program gave me was a set of tools with which I could begin to grow. I was never told that I could only use program resources in order to grow. My fellowship knows they are not the be-all-and-end-all. They encourage people to do or to be as much as they want to.

The first step of my program talks about powerless-ness. Step One requires the admission of powerlessness, while the remaining steps help me to live a better life—a life without active addiction. Step One is the only step that mentions a substance. The remaining steps exist to deal with personal growth—spiritual, physical, mental, emotional, social, and volitional. When I address each facet of my being and am able to achieve balance, life is better than I could have ever dreamed possible. It is through using the

Twelve Steps in everyday life that I can attain my own desired level of normalcy. There is no limit to how far I can grow.

My fellowship also provides me a place to try out new behaviors, actions, and thoughts. By attending meetings, I can share my thoughts and get feedback. If I can maintain an open mind and learn to take criticism constructively, I can learn about who I am with help from my peers, and I can do so in a safe environment. I talk with my sponsor and others in the program, and I am able to push myself to new limits. I learn to trust people and to trust my own thinking.

When I have opportunities for learning and growth, which some people choose to call problems, I think them over and try to solve them with advice from my sponsor. I make a habit of calling him on a daily basis. I mention anything I may have learned along the path of recovery. These conversations allow me to learn about my thought processes. If my solutions coincide with my sponsor's way of thinking, I can then begin to trust my decision-making. Prior to entering recovery, I trusted my own faulty thought processes. As others in the program have said, my best thinking usually got me into trouble, and my recovery depends on my ability to share my thoughts and concerns with my sponsor and to seek his advice.

Dictionary definitions of "normal" include words like "usual," "standard," "customary," "common," "average," and "typical." Philosophers and social scientists have spent countless hours and millions in grant money trying to define "normal." Maybe it's easier to define normal by thinking about what it is not, rather than what it is!

We do know that what's normal for one person may not be normal for another. Perception plays an important role in what seems normal. Each of us perceives normal differently. Perceptions come to us through our senses, but our understanding and expectations influence our perceptions. Since everyone's ability to perceive and understand how the world works is unique, everyone has different expectations, so naturally, everyone has the potential to see normal in a completely different light. It is no wonder that the world is full of people who seem so dissimilar.

Some people believe that chocolate ice cream is a delicious treat, while others think it is nothing special. (And some people have sensitive teeth, which makes eating ice cream very painful, if not impossible.) Some folks can smell a rose from twenty feet in a heavy wind, while others must practically stick their nose right in among the flower's petals to catch the scent. In either case the person doing the smelling may like or dislike the scent. Yet, in both of these cases, there is a norm. Chocolate ice cream has a taste that is normal for it, and a rose has a smell that is normal for it. If I placed a spoonful of chocolate ice cream in my mouth and tasted pastrami, or sniffed at a rose and smelled window cleaner, I would be concerned that the world had gone terribly wrong. What is normal is what we have learned to expect.

Back to those dictionary definitions. According to them, normal can mean "conforming to a standard," "adhering to a pattern," or "the usual or expected." Debating these definitions would be fruitless; I'll select the ones I found most useful in formulating my own definition and present them here.

In order to conform to a standard, the standard must be set and identifiable. The same is true for adhering to a pattern. Therefore, it should be safe to say that the usual becomes the expected, which becomes the standard or pattern. What *usually* happens is what I expect to happen. After a while, it simply becomes a pattern; I do this, and that happens. To me a standard is something I can rely on, something tested time and again that has always produced the same result. In the beginning, my using performed in this way. It was reliable in that it always made me feel better—except on those mornings after I drank too much. After a while, drugs and alcohol lost their reliability and the results of using became abnormal. Unfortunately, by the time this happened, I could not stop using. The abnormal had become normal in a weird, twisted sort of way.

When I began working, I learned what a normal day at work was like. While my normal day was much different from that of most people—most people do not build cars for a living—it was normal to me. If one day I woke up and drove to work, only to find that I was expected to do accounting, I'd consider that a departure from the norm. Things never got quite that weird at work, but I did have some very abnormal days during my time as an autoworker. For instance, I can remember times I went to work, expecting to report to my regular job, only to discover that I had been temporarily reassigned to another job on the assembly line. It was the same type of work; I was still building cars, but I was in a different department, in a different part of the building, working with different people, handling different parts, and so on. Sometimes I liked the change of assignment and sometimes I hated it. How I felt was determined by my expectations of what I thought was my normal job. Man is a creature of habit, and we tend to develop a comfort zone. We seek stability and don't like surprises. We do not expect the unexpected. We expect the normal, or what has become normal to us.

Normal is not always easy to pinpoint or describe. It varies from person to person, day to day, season to season, year to year, and understanding to understanding. Other potential variables include my patience, tolerance, and willingness to change. They all play a part in my understanding, as does my ability to be honest with myself, and to keep an open mind. Since normal is so hard to put a finger on and to hold in place, let us first look at some realistic ranges of normalcy. I live in lower Michigan. The common saying about the local weather is, "If you don't like it, wait fifteen minutes; it will change." Of course, that isn't literally true, but the weather can be rather fickle no matter where you live. Winter weather conditions in Michigan vary widely, depending on the area of the state. The snowfall can run from a few inches to a couple of feet each year in the south, to several feet in the north; along Lake Michigan or in the Upper Peninsula, grab your shovel—it's going to get deep. There is a wide range of temperatures as well. Still, each area of the state has a temperature range and an amount of snowfall that is considered normal.

Where I live, in the south central part of the state, winter usually begins sometime between late October and Thanksgiving. It does not let up until the middle of April, or sometimes as late as early May. It is normal during these times of the year to expect cold weather. Snow and cold are expected, and clouds seem to obscure the sun for the greater part of the winter season. January is usually very cold, and the temperatures can dip as low as zero-to-ten degrees Fahrenheit rather quickly.

The mercury can dip much lower, but that is not considered normal. Yet, if I venture outside in January and find the temperature is in the thirties, I think it is pretty much normal. After all, winter in Michigan is very cold. A particular winter day may not be as cold as I expect it to be in January, but it fits into my expectations of winter because I have a wide range of expectations for outdoor temperature built into my expectation of normal. When I am indoors, my expectations for the weather change dramatically. Expectations apply to all areas of my life.

For example, I have very strict expectations when I get into my car. I always expect it to start when I turn the key. If it does not start, look out; I may lose my grip on reality in a hurry. I also expect that when I put the gearshift into drive and step on the accelerator, the car will move forward. Then, I fully expect the brake pedal to bring me to a complete stop. In fact, I have come to expect these functions as being so normal that I am willing to bet my life on them—especially when it comes to the functioning of the brakes. If the car does not start or the accelerator does not move the car, I'm not leaving my driveway. However, if the brakes do not work after the accelerator has done its job, I am in big trouble. My expectation that the brakes will work is reasonable. I have developed this expectation over time. From the time I was young, I have ridden in cars, and the brakes have never failed, at least not yet. There have been some anxious stops due to snowy conditions, but those instances are exceptions, and they are not the fault of the brakes. They are the fault of the driver—and I always tend to give the driver a bit more leeway than I am willing to give the car, especially when the driver is me.

You can see that I have a wide range of expected normal with respect to the weather. However, regarding my car, that range quickly narrows. The same is true when it comes to my behavior. My range of acceptable normal behavior is much wider for myself than for others. For instance, when I am standing in line to pay for my goods and the cashier is taking his or her sweet time with the person in front of me, I can easily become annoyed and begin to think this behavior is other than normal. However, when I am the one working and someone mentions that I may be performing at below-average expectations, I am quick to come to my own defense. After all, I am working at a normal pace, carrying my normal workload.

What is normal in everyday life has a relatively similar range. A normal day is the same for most people. We get up, go to work or school, come home, eat dinner, perform some chores or participate in some recreational or leisure activities, watch some TV, and go to bed. It may sound boring when you think about it in this way, but it is normal nonetheless; it is the standard. In general, I consider a standard to be something I can rely on, like the brakes on my car—they generally perform as expected. However, normal seems to be much more expansive because, as the list of daily activities shows, there are many things that could be thrown in—or taken out—and the day could still be considered normal. Therefore, normal is, for the most part, what we understand as a range of acceptable behavior under a given set of circumstances.

In order to determine what is normal, I must make comparisons. Then I must make judgments based upon these comparisons. I do this every day. I make these comparisons with little or no detrimental effects to myself or to others. I go about my day ensuring that things go pretty much as planned. The house is still standing, the water for my shower is the proper temperature, the refrigerator has kept things fresh for me so I can make my breakfast, the stove will heat my food if I decide to cook, and my car starts so I can drive to work. Along my daily journey, I make comparisons at many points. If my car didn't start, it would fall outside the bounds of normal, and my day would be upset to some degree. I would almost automatically take action to bring things back to what I consider normal, and I would do this to regain my expected level of comfort. I like things to be normal for the most part, so I naturally struggle to maintain a level of normalcy in my life.

Who really defines what is normal? For most of my life, I seemed to allow my parents, my teachers, the news media, and others to shape my definition of normal. If I was not allowing others to shape my definition, I certainly was not taking the time or making the effort to discover my *own* definition. I simply lived with a decision made at some time and place in my past that told me that I was not normal or that I didn't fit in. This was an extremely unhealthy way for me to look at life. I no longer allow others to define what I believe to be normal, and I have begun to take a serious look at what I perceive as normal.

For example, it is normal for the United States of America to have a president. At one time, I thought it was normal to think that becoming president was a realistically obtainable goal. (While I would have to admit that it is normal to have a president, I must also admit that becoming president is not very normal at all.) As of this writing, the current president is only the forty-fourth person in the history of our country to hold the office. Forty-four people—forty-four men, actually—in more than 230 years is an extremely small number out of the total population of this country, especially when you consider the number of Americans who have lived throughout that time. Hundreds of millions of people have lived their lives in America since it was established as a country, and only forty-four of them have served as president. So, becoming president is not within the normal range of aspirations for most Americans, and never has been in our country's history. This example is one of many instances in which I used to assume a highly unusual event was actually normal and attainable.

Becoming a star athlete is another useful example. There are very few people who can actually make it to the professional sports level. A similarly small number achieve rock- or movie-star status. Even the number of doctors in this country is relatively low compared to the population in general. Yet there was a time when I believed that achieving any of these careers was practical and attainable—in a word, normal. I cannot explain my former belief. I can tell you that while I now understand that reaching these levels of fame and fortune is possible, I no longer see doing so as "normal." I now see it as extraordinary, more uncommon than normal. Like climbing one of the world's great mountains, reaching these positions in life is possible only for a few people, because it is out of the ordinary for people to possess the skills and desires necessary to attain such lofty heights.

What is more normal and more reachable to the average person is more in the mainstream. Most people simply do not have the desire to push themselves to their physical, mental, emotional, and spiritual limits, at least not enough so as to sustain the level of effort required to reach, and maintain, the high level of performance required by the demanding jobs listed above (and the list could be much longer). When I was young, I wanted to be president, or a firefighter, a police officer, or a doctor. I was taught that I could do anything I wanted, and I figured these were all normal things that could happen to me. You may have a similar list of things you wanted to be when you grew up. If you are like me (that is to say, normal), you probably didn't grow up to be any of the things on your list, either; and that's okay.

We all know we have to work for the things we want in life, but I did not understand this at first. Just as I used to think that becoming the president, or a doctor, or a firefighter, etc., would "happen" to me, I used to think other things also happened to me. Now I understand cause and effect. I understand that my actions cause what happens in my life, both the good and the bad. But this understanding took some time. Once I fully understood this concept, I could do something about my life, such as change my definition of normal.

It took some time, but I have redefined my understanding of normal. I now believe that *everybody defines normal for themselves*. Normal, once defined, becomes part of my new belief system, which in turn dictates my actions. My actions will determine the consequences. I have learned that consequences are not always negative. They are simply the next step in the process of life. They are not punishments or rewards; they are perfectly impersonal and just and are perfectly normal.

Quite often I know what the consequences of an action will be before I act. If I fail to put gasoline in my car I will eventually become stranded in a place where I do not want to be. I know if I put my trash out on trash day, it will "magically disappear" and I won't have to put up with the smell of rotting garbage. I know these things. They are part of life. Every day is full of things that happen very naturally—very normally. You could say that recurrence is what defines my new normal.

I now include myself in my new definition of normal. What a concept! Everybody else is just as normal as I am today. I came to this new definition by simply looking deeply into who I am, what I like and dislike, what I want and need, and how I look, think, act and feel, and have decided to include me in what I believe to be normal.

Since I have come to the conclusion that I am normal, what does that make everyone else? I now believe that everyone is normal in his or her own way. We all have talents, abilities, character defects, and shortcomings. Everyone acts a little goofy from time to time. What's the big deal? After all, if I can be normal, *anybody* can be normal. To those whose achievements make them seem like they are "above" normal, like those listed above, I now give the title of "extraordinary" or "exceptional." This is a very simple way to be inclusive. No one is actually above or below normal; some people simply scale greater heights. I thank God for every one of the exceptional or extraordinary people in our world. These extraordinary people gave me electricity, fast transportation (on and off the ground), refrigeration, and all the modern conveniences I rely on today. However, just because these people reach heights I have neither attained nor wish to reach, they are not any more or less normal than I am. They still have to sleep, eat, drink, wear clothes, shave, shower, brush their teeth, and so on. When I boil it all down, we have much more in common than not. They are simply normal people who have achieved extraordinary accomplishments. If I continued to spend my time and energy getting drunk or high, I would not be able to achieve anything extraordinary. As my life improves, extraordinary can become more ordinary. Extraordinary can become normal. Wouldn't it be great if everyone were extraordinary? Well, maybe everyone is.

If everyone is normal—including extraordinary and exceptional people—then anyone can be normal. Understanding this, I simply cannot exclude myself from my growing list of normal people, and neither should you. The extraordinary and exceptional people are normal, too, and without them we would have no presidents, no doctors or nurses, and none of the things that make life so convenient. Life would be rough. In fact, we might still be living in caves, because no one would have been extraordinary enough to venture into a new way of life. As I celebrate my newfound normalcy, I celebrate the extraordinary people who have come before me, who are here now, and who will come later. I celebrate just how normal and how human we all are.

I have stopped thinking of normal as some perfect person, place, or ideal. Normal is right here, right now. I must learn to embrace life and live with normal on a daily basis. If I see normal as what other people are and I am not, then I cause myself unnecessary suffering. When I feel abnormal, I struggle to gain normalcy. When I struggle, I am uncomfortable. When I am uncomfortable, I seek comfort. When comfort is unattainable, suffering is unending. I did not enter recovery to be unhappy and uncomfortable. I entered recovery to get away from that misery, not to wallow in it. To be completely honest, if I had to live in misery I would probably go back to drinking, because "what's the point?" When I drank, at least I knew to expect more misery and more drinking as the vicious cycle continued. Since I no longer drink or drug, I deserve something better. I want to be happy, comfortable, and serene.

Normal is not a form of perfection. Perfection cannot be found on this planet. Nobody is perfect, even all those "perfect people" I used to see everywhere. Normal is not what I want to be; normal is what I am right now! I can take normal with me everywhere I go, and I should, because it is important to be happy and serene, and I can do that if I feel normal. Perfection is not only out of reach; it is crazy to strive for it because if I could somehow reach perfection,

I would still not be normal. I would not fit in and I would end up starting the whole cycle all over again.

Probably the biggest fib I have ever been told is: "Practice makes perfect." Nothing makes perfect. Here is the plain truth: "Practice makes progress." As long as I practice things every day, like brushing my teeth and doing my job, I will become more fluent in the things I choose to practice. What I should focus on practicing are those things I want to become better at doing. When I say focus, I mean think about what I am doing while I am doing it; it is thought coupled with action.

What do you think about when you are performing the very normal action of brushing your teeth? If you are thinking about other things, you are practicing that as a brushing habit. It will become your normal way of brushing your teeth. If, for example, I decided that from now on, when I brush my teeth, I am going to count the number of strokes I provide for each set of teeth to be sure that all of my teeth get a certain number of strokes, I could do that with ease. It would require only that I make a small change in the way I perform a small chore. Since it is something I do a couple of times a day, over time I could easily adopt this new habit. This new normal way of brushing my teeth would become so automatic that soon I would be doing it without even thinking. I no longer think about how I brush my teeth. Most people don't. (This isn't really a big deal as long as your teeth get clean!)

Tooth brushing is a positive habit; however, we often do things out of habit that affect our lives in negative ways. We need to stop to think about *what we are not thinking about*—and then think about it. Put another way, we must consciously develop an awareness of our actions. Humans are creatures of habit, and becoming aware of our habits is a skill that takes time to develop.

Once I realized this and began to become aware of my habits, I found that my brain remained on autopilot during habitual activities, so I started telling it what to think about and when. One of the directions I gave it was to start watching what I was not thinking about and not consciously thinking about, before taking action. I began to see that some amazing things had been happening without my conscious consent. Some of my thoughts and actions had become so automatic that I was not consciously aware of what I was doing, and so did not act in the manner I really wanted. One automatic tendency I discovered was giving other people credit as being normal for things that are not really too normal, at least not for me. One of these things falls directly into what I call the "Normie versus Alkie Syndrome": the idea that being able to consume alcohol without consequences is normal.

Normal is different from one person to another, and we all decide what is normal for ourselves. Put another way, we decide that we can decide for ourselves. In accepting this one simple yet extremely important idea, we have made progress toward becoming normal. There is still work to be done, because we may need to redefine what normal really is, and if we are able do this we will become uncomfortable until we become accustomed to our new normal. My new normal includes not drinking alcohol or using other drugs. You can choose a new normal as well. I have chosen this new way of life and I cherish it. I want and need to protect my new sense of normalcy. However, I did not reach this new normal overnight. There was a process involved, a process that I was not even aware existed. It was a type of covert operation that took place in my head, my heart, and my soul. The process was assisted by my sponsor and those I trust in my program. The process surprised me. One day I realized my attitude about drinking had changed. Here's how:

One Sunday afternoon I went to my brother and sister-in-law's house for dinner. My brother is a talented cook; his wife does all the clean-up, and all I have to do is show up and eat. It's a great deal for me, and it's one I accept whenever they offer it, which they do on a regular basis. On this particular occasion they served spaghetti with all the trimmings, including a bottle of wine. When we sat down to eat, my sister-in-law began to pour herself a glass of wine, hesitated noticeably, looked at me with an "I've been so thoughtless" expression, and then asked, "Would it bother you if we had wine with our dinner?"

I was relatively new to recovery, and this was not something I expected. My sister-in-law hadn't been thinking about drinking; she doesn't have to. She isn't alcoholic, and neither is my brother. They drink when they want, and stop when they think they have had enough, if not before. They are social drinkers. They planned to have wine with their dinner. They invited me without thinking about how my recovery would affect them. My sister-in-law began to pour herself a glass of wine—a perfectly normal thing for her to do—and suddenly realized it might not be a good idea because I was there.

I felt I had to answer her question, so I said "no" without thinking. I continued, saying, "It doesn't bother me if you drink. It only bothers me if I drink." Now, as I mentioned, I answered without thinking. I had practiced not drinking for a relatively short time, yet the results had far-reaching effects. My subconscious thought process began to take in the new knowledge that I didn't drink because it bothered me to drink. This was a major shift in my thinking, and, in this case, it happened very naturally—so naturally, in fact, that I didn't even notice what had happened until later that evening. My sister-in-law and I exchanged a couple of quick comments concerning alcohol, and then we went about having dinner. She poured herself and my brother some wine, I drank my soda, and we had a pleasant, unremarkable evening—unremarkable, that is, except for the lesson I was to learn from the event. Those two little sentences exchanged at dinner with my sister-in-law radically changed my view of what is normal and what is not when it comes to people.

People come in all shapes, sizes, looks, styles, colors, and types. I don't understand people—probably most people. I do my best to be an understanding person, but I simply cannot understand why people do some of the things they do. Almost every day, I see people do things that baffle me. They pull out in front of me in traffic, treat their children in ways I could interpret as insane, and cross the street without looking because a sign says the pedestrians have the right-of-way. I don't get it. But I don't have to understand them for them to be normal. And it is not my place to understand everything. I must simply accept those things I don't understand or would not do, those I believe I am unable to do, or those I simply choose not to do as being quite normal for other people.

Some people drink alcoholic beverages or use other drugs recreationally. I used to, but I no longer partake in these practices. The reason I quit has to do with the direction my life was headed. Using had consequences that became so intensely negative that I had to quit. Using in any way, even ways that did not result in my becoming completely loaded, became unacceptable to me; I realized it was abuse. It was when I discovered my new definition of abuse that I realized I might have a problem. My point is that many people don't have the problem that I have. While this fact may not be a revelation to you, it may come as a surprise to you to realize that you may think of those people, of them, as being normal *because* they can drink. If you do, I beg of you to change your thinking in this matter. Maybe you don't think of social use of alcohol or other drugs as "the norm." However, many people do, and to their own detriment. After all, if that is the norm, how can I ever possibly fit in, or be normal, myself? This idea is as dangerous to my personal growth as playing with dynamite, yet I see evidence that some people believe this mythological notion.

I cannot count the number of times I have heard others say something that sounds like "I went to a party last weekend with a bunch of normal people." When I hear this sentiment shared it makes my skin crawl, because I used to say the same thing; I used to call other people normal without thinking about what I was implying about myself. I used to say this without thinking. In early recovery, I had heard enough other people say it that it seemed acceptable. I no longer feel that way. I no longer consider it acceptable to regard other people as normal (or more normal than I regard myself) simply because they can consume alcohol without suffering horrible consequences.

During my using years I thought of myself as an alcoholic, and I felt that I wasn't normal. In fact, that was true; I was far from normal. Drinking and using as I did was about as far from normal as a person can get. It was certainly as far from normal as I ever care to be. I never want to be in that place again. However, I don't drink anymore—not that *not* drinking makes me somehow normal. Not drinking gives me a chance to become normal again—assuming I was ever normal to begin with—and I think I was normal at some point. (One may have to go all the way back to the cradle to pinpoint one's normal, but it can be found.)

We conformed to a standard, adhered to a pattern, did the usual or expected at some point in our lives. How hard is it to be a normal baby? What do we really expect of an infant? They cry, someone feeds them, they sleep, and they need to be changed and held. I did those things when I was an infant. I must have been normal back then, even if I lost my sense of normalcy shortly out of the crib! The point is that I *did* lose my sense of normalcy somewhere along the line. I drank like a drunk. My life became unmanageable. I was able to admit I had a problem and sought help. When I sought help, it was there waiting. I stopped drinking. At this point in my recovery, it would be easy to say I am still far from normal, and I might agree with this statement on some level. Still, calling other people normal because they can drink annoys me so deeply.

Calling other people normal—and considering myself not-so-normal—started driving me out of my sense of serenity, because I can't drink and have a normal life. When I drink, I suffer badly, and all too often so do the people around me. Drinking simply is not part of a normal life for me. In fact, drinking doesn't make anybody normal. In fact, there is no one thing (outside of general bodily functions) that anyone does that makes them more normal than anybody else. Eating, drinking (nonalcoholic beverages), sleeping, etc.—these are normal to everyone. Very little else is considered normal to everyone. My normal now includes not drinking. Other people's normal includes drinking. I now believe we can celebrate the differences. I can learn from them and grow with them. But first, I have to get over the hang-ups I have with the fact that some people can drink alcohol without suffering terrible side effects, while I have terrible side effects if I consume it. It's not my job to understand why I have side effects. I only have to accept the truth and move on with my life.

I refuse to take certain medications because they have very bad side effects—the side effects are worse than the illnesses they are supposed to cure. I don't think twice about this. When I have a cold, I take a certain kind of cold medication. I take it because, through trial and error, I have found it to be effective for me. I quit taking the ones that did not work for me or made me feel worse. Why? I quit because it made sense for me to do so. I decided that I didn't like the negative side effects I got from taking the medication, so I quit taking it. I didn't have to understand why it made me feel poorly; I simply accepted that it did and moved on.

Although it was a form of self-delusion, I used this same approach with certain types of alcohol during my using years. I quit drinking tequila because (I thought) it almost killed me. Even though I drank for many more years, I never drank tequila again. Peppermint schnapps also made the list of alcohols I never drank.

Then, one day, I discovered that it wasn't the tequila, schnapps, whiskey, pot, wine, coke, or beer that was killing me. It was the addict in me that was causing all the undesirable side effects. Using these various substances made me miserable. I could start using, but I could not stop. When it came to drinking, my brakes—my ability to stop—failed on a regular basis. Eventually, I made the decision to quit drinking altogether. Like all the other medications I have on my "do not take" list, alcohol and other drugs have a new place of residence in my life.

I no longer need to know why certain substances disagree with me, any more than I need to know why the other medications I do not use disagree with me. I only need to remember that *I do not pick up a drink or a drug*.

While not drinking has become part of my new normal, I do not begrudge people who can drink. Why should I? I don't begrudge people who can take Tylenol. I simply do not take it myself. I do not take Tylenol and I do not drink alcohol; it is that simple. Like I told my sister-in-law, it doesn't bother me if *you* drink; it only bothers me if *I* drink. Today I choose not to be bothered.

I had to stop the us-and-them mentality. It is this exact thought process that has caused me great mental anguish. If I allow them to be normal because they can drink, I am certainly harboring a desire to drink, to be like them, and to fit in. I can no longer afford to drink. My life is too good today to give it all up to drinking and drugging. Therefore, I must become more accepting of the way other people are, especially when it comes to drinking alcohol or using drugs recreationally. Some people drink; I don't. Some people use; I don't. That is the way of the world. Making not drinking or drugging part of my new normal makes life easier to live, even though others may choose to drink. However, if I categorize people as *us* and *them*, or *them* and *me*, I alienate myself from a large part of society, making it impossible to fit in with people outside the program. Instead, I choose to be part of society. I do my part by choosing not to drink.

Only a small fraction of those who need help with various addictions are actually in a program and fellowship of recovery. To set myself apart from people outside my program puts severe and possibly damaging limits on my personal growth. I once tended to walk around in life, except in meetings, not knowing how to act. I tried to fit into a world where I felt I didn't belong. If the only place I feel I really belong is in a twelve-step meeting, I must change this attitude in order to continue to grow and function in the world.

What I have found is that my fellowship is a safe place. When I first entered recovery I needed to feel a sense of belonging, and I received much more than that in the meetings I attended. I felt a safe sense of belonging, love, caring, and empathy. In the selfless acts of caring provided by program members I found the help I needed to take the steps necessary to begin my recovery. I found a positive "we" in my life. "We" helped me to get started and was necessary for the rest of my recovery. "We" helps me grow by continuing to provide a safe place to try out new behaviors without feeling like I am being judged too harshly. I did some stupid things within the safety of my program and watched others shrug them off while continuing to go about their business. They did not make a big deal out the stupid things I did, and neither should I.

The real world is chock-full of the same kinds of behaviors that exist within my program. In fact, I have found that my fellowship is really just a mirror image of the world at large. The difference is that in my fellowship I share the view in the mirror with people with whom I am comfortable, people I understand and trust, and who understand and trust me. I can be comfortable with people who are not in recovery. When I say comfortable, I am talking about not thinking in terms of in or out of the program, drinker or nondrinker, or anything that sets me apart from "them." This feeling of understanding, acceptance, and serenity takes time to develop, but I am making steady progress.

I have grown to think of myself simply as a person. I can fit in anywhere. I can go anywhere, see anything, say anything, and do anything except consume alcohol or other drugs. On top of that, I have discovered that I can learn from anybody, as long as I am willing to learn. After all, if I limit my learning to things I gather only in the program, I put restrictions on myself. If I limit my activities to program activities, I restrict my life. I did not enter recovery to put restrictions on myself. I entered recovery to remove restrictions, to get rid of misery. I entered recovery to be "happy, joyous, and free." My new freedom includes activities of all kinds, with people of all kinds, in places of all kinds, for reasons of all kinds. It takes work, but it is definitely worth it.

Much seems to depend on how I look at any situation. There are many people in the world who can drink or use without suffering horrible consequences. I can choose to set myself apart from them if I so desire. However, if I do so, I exclude millions of potential friends and acquaintances from my life, to forgo possible learning and potential growth. I can accept that since they don't have to drink when we go out for dinner, they can drink at dinner, or they may not. I go places with so-called normies on a regular basis.

The places we go serve alcohol, and my friends just as easily order alcoholic or nonalcoholic beverages. Their choice to order nonalcoholic beverages is perfectly normal for them. My old thinking tells me they will order a beer just because they can. However, they may not be in the mood for alcohol and choose not to order it. I regularly go to restaurants that serve alcohol—with a friend who has no problem with alcohol—and he or she chooses to order a soft drink or a glass of iced tea. Even if he or she does order a beer, it doesn't bother me because it only bothers me if I drink, and I don't drink because drinking makes me abnormal. I have no trouble watching another person consume an alcoholic beverage.

While I have excluded alcohol from my diet, I have not excluded people from my life. I like most people. I used to like alcohol. I choose to exclude alcohol from my life just as I choose to exclude certain people from my life. As long as I do not drink, I can invite some very interesting people into my life, and they can invite me into theirs. It is a win-win situation. I choose not to drink and I enjoy the company of others, some of whom choose to drink and others who do not.

Why is it that seeing a disgustingly drunken person does not make me want to drink, but seeing people enjoy alcohol causes me discomfort? Some might say this is because seeing the disgustingly drunk person reminds me of where I have been. I would tend to agree. However, I have also enjoyed alcohol. I used to love to drink. If I am completely honest, and I try to be, I'll admit I would enjoy being able to drink today. By that I mean I wish I were able to drink without all those unsightly and dire consequences. Unfortunately, when I drink, I end up like the disgusting drunk. Still, why should I begrudge someone else the pleasure of enjoying a cocktail? I don't begrudge people what they have in their lives: their jobs, spouses, children, money, cars, etc. (At least if I am living the program, I don't begrudge people these things.) Then why would I begrudge their desire or ability to drink alcohol? My guess is that it is because I would enjoy being able to drink today without all those terrible consequences. However, it is long past time for me to stop wishing things were different and accept the fact that some people can have alcohol, while I choose not to do so today. After all, using for me is now a matter of choice. I could drink a beer with them. But I know where I would end up, even though I don't know what the long-term results might be. Because of this uncertainty, I choose not to drink. I do this because I don't want to be abnormal anymore, and when I don't drink I can be as normal as anybody else. While I can honestly say that I would enjoy being able to drink or use socially, I know the reality of my disease, and I no longer choose the path that leads to abnormal behavior. The power to choose is wonderful.

There are many who choose not to partake in alcoholic beverages. There are more of them making this choice, more people who are not addicts, than there are people who are addicts in recovery. (Studies show that approximately one-third of the population in the United States does not drink alcoholic beverages.) A little math puts the number of nondrinkers in this country somewhere around one hundred million people. One hundred million is a large number of nondrinkers. For whatever reason, one out of three people does not drink. Researching this information helped me drive home the point for myself. One hundred million people in this country are not drinking. This statistic made me dizzy while I was trying to take it all in. It gave me a different perspective on the "drinking/not drinking dilemma" that I used to dwell on. I used to think everybody drank or used socially, was in recovery, or was an addict or a drunk. This new information helped me to see things in an entirely different light.

I no longer see normies and those in recovery. I see people in and out of the program. This makes for an important shift in my attitude about life. Social users and nonusers are people who are outside the program. The person who is still getting loaded is also outside the program. According to the primary purpose of my twelve-step program, I am supposed to help those who wish to recover from their addiction. However, I recall nothing in the program that says I should exclude other nondrinkers or social drinkers from my life. In fact, program literature talks about how, once I begin practicing the program, I can go anywhere and do anything if I am spiritually fit. Now that I do my best to stay spiritually fit, I can participate in life. Today I participate in life and see it as a completely normal thing to do.

"When I don't drink, I can be as normal as anybody else." This is a direct quote from my first sponsor. When he first mentioned it to me, it flew over my head. I thought that being alcoholic made me different from others and that I would be different for the rest of my life. However, I have come to understand that everybody has troubles and issues. We are all normal in some areas and not so normal in others; drinking has nothing to do with being normal. I have talked with many people who have no problem drinking alcohol. They also have crazy ideas, just as I do. They just don't act on them. When I drank and drugged, I used to act on any thought that came into my head, as long as it "seemed like a good idea at the time." Today I don't do that. I take time to analyze the thought, the situation, even the consequences, before choosing to act. These are very normal activities. Giving other people credit for being normal because they do not drink leaves out all the possible difficulties they may have in their lives such as the illnesses they may have or the financial, family, or social demons they may encounter. These issues and concerns are not included in my equation or my understanding of what is normal.

Many people whom I consider normal have disorders that they believe make them different or abnormal, yet they somehow find ways to cope. There are so many diseases and disorders that I couldn't possibly list them all, but a short list could include such things as overeating, gambling, smoking, sexual issues, abuse against oneself or others, and posttraumatic stress disorder. Many of these examples are common manifestations of the disease of addiction while others are not. Let's not overlook cancer, diabetes, and other disorders of this ilk. These diseases may differ from addiction, but they nonetheless require a change in lifestyle not unlike what I have experienced. What makes these people seem normal is that they deal with these issues in more healthy ways than the ways I used to deal with my drinking. However, today I deal with my drinking in the healthiest way possible. I abstain and participate in a program that helps me learn to live a healthy and fulfilling life. While some people may not need, or use, a program to deal with their issues, many people like me do seek help. Seeking help for problems and issues we encounter is normal behavior. There are counselors, psychiatrists, and psychologists whose offices are full of those seeking help. There are many forms of help available for addiction, and there are many self-help groups. Self-help titles comprise a large portion of available titles. Bookstores would not sell them if people did not want them. We all need a little help now and then. My participating in a program to learn how to cope with life issues is no different from another person's use of self-help books or support groups.

As I see it, my fellowship mirrors life in general to allow for me to try out new thoughts and behaviors in a safe haven before I attempt them in the world at large. I sought and received help for my problem from my fellowship. What I didn't expect was all the other support I received, both directly and indirectly. When I look at others in the program I see that they come from different walks of life, have all kinds of issues, differ in their willingness to try new things, and have big and small goals. Regardless of who or what they are, they all have one thing in common: They sit at the tables and seek help just like me.

My sponsor once told me that if you clean up a horse thief, you just have a clean horse thief, unless they decide to stop stealing horses. There are people, supposedly in recovery, who still lie, cheat, and steal. They have yet to discover how these activities hurt them and others. Hopefully, they will decide to change their behaviors if and when they are able to see the truth. However, there are people who do not have addiction and who also perform some pretty awful acts against their fellow man, for example, some members of the clergy. They are considered examples of what is just and right. Yet many of them are alleged to have abused children, stolen, or committed other crimes. It is true that no one is perfect.

In my fellowship I get a small snapshot of the outside world, and I am able to test new behaviors in an environment conducive to my personal growth. Then, the real test of my new behavior comes when I venture into the world outside the protected walls of my fellowship.

Once I heard a story about a man who was running late for church. Upon arriving at the church, he noticed everyone leaving. He got the attention of an elderly woman and asked if he had missed the sermon, to which she replied, "Sir, the sermon is just beginning." So the man ran inside to hear what the pastor was saying, only to find the church entirely empty. The man came back outside, disgruntled, to find the little woman sitting at the bus stop. As he approached the woman, he stated, "I thought you said the sermon had just begun." "Oh, but it has," she replied. "The preacher said his piece and he is done with that. Now it is up to each of us to see how we can apply what we learned to our everyday lives. That is where the sermon really takes place."

My program is a lot like the sermon. I go to meetings to learn. Then I apply what I have learned to my everyday life. That is where my program really lives—in my everyday life. What my program really does is allow me to see who and what I really am. This allows me to change the things I find objectionable. I make these changes with continued practice, with the help of people I have come to trust in the program, and most of all, with the help of God as I have come to understand Him. However, to make any changes, *I must take action.*

While I was active in my disease, I was not living life. I was, at best, existing. I took no action to make things better—for myself or for others. Since I have entered recovery, I have learned it is up to me to change me. I receive a great deal of help from those I meet in my program, but they are unable to fix my life. Only I can change me, through taking action. Even God is not able to change me if all I do is stay where I am, especially if my inertia is the result of being an addict. I have to take the necessary steps if I am to get anywhere.

I must participate in my recovery and in life. I must take action to apply the things I have learned in meetings, through reading and discussing the basic text of my fellowship, through talking with my sponsor, and by getting in touch with my conscience. For the most part I believe I know right from wrong, but some issues require more knowledge than I possess, or more wisdom than I am able to muster or exhibit. The program is there to help me with these things, yet it is up to me to take the necessary steps to better myself. The reward is nearly always worth more than the work involved. I can become involved in life; I can participate in the activities of living instead of plowing through the misery of dying the death of an addict.

Life is really one big, long process. It is made up of many smaller processes, but life is still a process. Once I begin to live my recovery, it becomes my mission to determine how much I want to participate in the process. I can be part of the action, or I can sit in the stands and watch. Neither is more important in and of itself, but I need to determine which makes me happy—or happier. If I simply "don't use, and go to meetings," that is what I will get out of the program: I'll simply be abstinent at a meeting. However, if I want to experience all the opportunity life has to offer, I need to take more action.

When I met my first sponsor I was just four days out of rehab, but I knew I wanted something he had. He was happy. That was all I noticed at first, although I came to learn that he had much more than just happiness. I decided I wanted all that he had to offer. He was "happy, joyous, and free," as is said in the fellowship. He had serenity, courage, and wisdom. I jokingly told him I was going to steal everything he had so I could use it myself. He told me that I could not steal that which was freely given. He wanted to share what he had with others if they were willing to do their part. If I was willing to participate in my own growth, he was willing to give me everything he had. What he had was all the knowledge he had gained in his ninety-plus years of life, most of which had been spent in recovery. He told me that all I had to do to get what he had was to do what he did to get it. A good friend of mine likes to say, "This is not Triple-A; nobody's going to tow you through it." I have found this to be true. The more I participate, the more I grow. The more I grow, the more I want to participate. Recovery is the opposite of the downward spiral I used to live in, and it is very exciting.

The most important thing I have discovered about taking part in my recovery is that I can be as normal as anybody. Whether someone is in the program, drinks socially, or simply chooses not to drink, they are no more normal than I am, and I am no less normal than they are. That is the gift of my recovery, and it can be your gift as well, but only if you work for what you want.

My plan to become normal, insofar as I had a plan, was inspired by my first sponsor. He taught me so much, and I know I can never repay him directly. Instead, as the program teaches, I choose to "pay it forward," to help others in the same way he helped me. It is what he would have wanted me to do.

"Take what you can use, and leave the rest behind"; that's what members of my fellowship say. However, I suspect that there is very little that I will ever want to leave behind. My first sponsor taught me so much, as have others in my recovery. I've come to refer to this process as "improvement." We can all choose to improve our lives, and you can choose to improve yours.

EACH PERSON'S BOTTOM IS AN

INDIVIDUAL UNDERSTANDING.

NO TWO ARE EXACTLY THE

SAME. EACH PERSON IN

RECOVERY HAS "PAID THE

PRICE OF ADMISSION." SOME

HAVE PAID MORE, SOME HAVE

PAID LESS, BUT EACH ONE

HAS PAID A HEAVY PRICE

BEFORE ENTERING THE ROOMS

OF RECOVERY AND TAKING HIS

OR HER PLACE AT THE TABLE.

3

COMPARING

Comparing is a huge part of life; in fact, I compare all the time. From the time I crawl out of bed in the morning until I make my way back there at night, I compare. I might be described as a "compulsive comparer." I can't seem to help myself. I believe some of my comparing is necessary; however, I must be careful, because it is all too easy to begin believing all of my comparisons are necessary. Many are not, and are actually harmful to my personal growth.

I compare to determine what I believe to be good or bad, right or wrong. I consider comparisons to be a useful part of life when used correctly. After all, I must make decisions in my life, and to do so I must compare my alternatives. When I make a simple decision, such as whether to shower in the morning, the mental comparison between the advantages of doing so and the disadvantages of not doing so happens so quickly that I hardly notice. This comparison is required to live a happy and healthy life. I'm happier going out in public when I know I've had a shower. (And so is the public!)

Like anything else, comparing can be taken to extremes. I have found this to be the case whenever comparing impedes my life, my personal growth, or my general happiness. There are other reasons to not overcompare, but I like to keep things simple. I usually go to extremes when comparing myself to others.

It is easy to compare myself with others without even thinking about it. I find myself doing it all the time. While walking down the street, I sometimes find myself thinking I am different from others simply because they look different. They may look happier, more content, more relaxed, or more stressed or upset, or I may simply think they are better- (or worse-) looking than I am. I find it difficult—sometimes impossible—not to make these comparisons. This thinking can be damaging to my personal growth. If I feel that someone else is better or worse than I am—for any reason—I can cause emotional harm to myself, destroying my serenity and jeopardizing my recovery.

I rarely compare myself to someone else only to find we are the same. I always consider myself to be either better than or worse than the person to whom I compare myself.

I often feel inferior to others. It is easy for me to understand how this kind of thinking can undermine my personal growth. I make myself feel low and kick myself while I am "down." In the process, I reduce my self-esteem to even lower levels and can easily reach the point where I consider life not worth living. I can also convince myself that I might as well get drunk, because "What's the use?"

Even if I don't allow my feelings to sink to such depths, when my self-esteem takes a beating such as this, the results are usually very negative. Feeling inferior to others can cause me to make bad decisions in order to make myself feel better or not to feel at all. When I give myself less credit than I give others, I question my own self-worth. I wonder if my opinion is worth sharing with others. Worse yet, I might wonder if my opinion is worth considering even for myself. I begin to doubt my own thinking, and in the process I limit any potential for growth that might have occurred if I'd thought things through on my own. Using my God-given brain for its intended purpose can be a daunting task. At times I slow or even stop my recovery, but I do not pick up. Every minute I spend comparing myself with others and doubting my own thinking is one less minute I can enjoy life. While this way of thinking isn't the end of the world, it hinders my recovery and negatively impacts my life.

When I feel inferior, I often lash out at others by talking negatively about them or cutting them down in order to make myself feel superior. Although I actually feel less of a person than I think they are, I do what I can to elevate myself to a level above them. While this might work temporarily, it is harmful. I must avoid it, because I will realize what I have been doing and I will usually end up feeling guilty. I then begin to feel "worse than," and the self-perpetuating cycle can start all over again. This vicious downward spiral can repeat itself again and again, and can hinder any real progress toward becoming the person I truly want to be.

On the other hand, while feeling better than another person feeds my ego, making me feel better about myself, it can be just as damaging as feeling inferior to or worse than another person. Feeling better than another person leads to another variety of inferior-feelings, whereby I eventually begin to feel bad about myself for feeling superior. I have also found another effect of ego-feeding to be a more subtle foe; when I feel I am better than another person, it is easy to continue to feed this feeling and eventually find ways to feel superior to nearly everyone. I have found that I can actually do this to such extremes that I find myself thinking I am above my boss, pastor, therapist, parents, sponsor, or even God Himself.

While I rarely get so carried away with this form of comparing that I think of myself as better than God, the damage begins long before I get to that point. Once I begin to feel I am superior to other people, it is easy to convince myself that they are the ones who need improvement—not me. After all, they are beneath me. They must work to attain my level of greatness. Following this line of thought can cause me to believe that I do not need improvement. Although I know that the day I no longer need to improve will be the day they throw dirt on my coffin, I can easily convince myself that since I am better than other people, I can rest on my past accomplishments. When I begin to believe this self-propaganda, I stop practicing the things that have helped me make the improvements necessary to get to this point. At best, I continue without growing. Even worse, I can move backward in my development or backslide, as some people call it. If I allow this backward momentum to continue, I can easily lose ground I will later discover I can ill afford to lose.

Overcoming fear, trying out new behavior, and learning new things are not natural, easy things for me to do. Sometimes the work I must do to make a positive change in my life is exhausting. I owe it to myself to hold onto the progress I have made. Therefore, I have found it wise to stop comparing myself to other people for any reason. While we are all different, no one is inherently better than, or worse than, any other person. This understanding can be difficult to grasp. I wrestle with it often, as do others, but I think everyone struggles with it to some degree.

Today I categorize myself as an addict without comparing myself to others. When I first entered recovery, I compared my using habits with those of others. But I have outgrown that now. I got tired of trying to decide whether I had used more or less than other people, of comparing my "bottom" experience to that of others.

A "bottom" is the point of desperation that makes an addict realize that "enough is enough" and that recovery is the only option other than jails, hospitals, or death. It is the realization that something must give and that there is nowhere else to go, that there are no more avenues to explore. Call it what you will; each person's bottom is an individual understanding. No two are exactly the same. Each person in recovery has "paid the price of admission." Some have paid more, some have paid less, but each one has paid a heavy price before entering the rooms of recovery and taking his or her place at the table. Some believe that until an addict has hit bottom, he or she is not willing or able to reach out for help. Those who are unsure if they have reached their bottom are encouraged to continue attending meetings and learning from others without worrying too much about whether or not they have reached their bottom. Sadly, some choose to explore whether they can pick up again, because they are unconvinced. Some of these people do find their way back to recovery and others do not, but that is the nature of the disease of addiction. Many people use comparison to justify their continued using; as

I once did. They seem to think along the lines of "I am not that bad yet."

For some reason I thought the lower the bottom, the cooler the person. However, I came to believe that not only is this kind of thinking foolish, but it borders on the insane. Just because she drank for more years, he used more per day, or she got into more trouble, they are no better than or worse than anybody else. They are only different. If they are in a meeting, odds are that they are alcoholics or addicts, just like me. If they decide they are, they are. That is enough for me today. I don't care how addicted they are, because being an addict is like being pregnant; you either are or you aren't. There is no "I am a little bit alcoholic." I have heard people say, "He has a little drinking problem," but I have never heard anybody say, "He is kind of, sort of, an alcoholic" or "He is a little bit of an addict." I either am or I am not when it comes to my disease. Once I admit to myself that I am an addict—once I have decided to believe the truth and ask for help—I can then begin the recovery process.

Recovery is a process. It is not contained in some magic pill. Some people are farther along in the process than others. When I first entered recovery, I thought I would never become a "long-timer." (There is still a chance I won't, since I have not yet reached that point.) I am in no real hurry to age; however, I do hope to become a person with long-term recovery. I am content to let that happen normally. Because recovery is a process, I am learning to let people be where they are without judging them to be better off or worse off than I am. Wherever they are in the process, I can learn from them if I am paying attention and am willing to learn. Consequently, I compare less, relate more, and do my best to learn from everybody, and I do it for my own good, not for anyone else's. I am often surprised at what I am able to learn. Profound wisdom can come from the most unlikely sources.

I have found that I need to allow other people to grow in their own good time. I must practice accepting others for who they are and for how far they have journeyed in their lives. I must mind my process and grow as I see fit. Some people are content with not drinking and going to meetings—that suits them just fine. Today I am okay with allowing others to follow their own path. I want to push as far as I can, learn all there is, grow as much as possible, and reach for the stars. I had to take a look at how much comparing I did, when I did it, how I did it, and most importantly, why I was doing it and to whom I was comparing myself.

I still catch myself comparing. I have found one comparison that can be catastrophic to my personal development. To categorize myself as an addict, but a social drinker, for example, as normal, is just plain insanity. This comparison must change in order for me to reach beyond my current limits, to go for the things I have told myself I could never have. Since I entered my recovery fellowship, I've realized that as long as I don't pick up, I can continue to be as normal as anyone.

My fellowship and my life really are mirrors of each other. People inside my program are very much like people outside my program. When I see someone on the street—unless I have met him or her in a meeting—I have no idea if he or she is involved in a recovery program. I never really considered this until I began looking for similarities between life in the program and life outside the program.

We all know some people in this world who act in ways that are beneficial to society at large, while others do things that are harmful. I used to be among the class that was harmful. However, I am no longer a user; I no longer victimize others for my own gain. That doesn't mean there are no longer people who victimize others. In fact, I can find these people wherever I go. There are even people in recovery who maraud around the program looking for their next victims, just as there are people who are not in recovery who take advantage of other people, places, and things in order to make personal gain. I have found this to be neither good nor bad in and of itself. It is simply something I must be aware of to avoid falling prey to one of their schemes. Sometimes I find myself hurt by someone else's actions. I am gullible at times, and I have found these times to be of profound importance to my life and my personal growth.

I have learned that when someone takes advantage of me in some way, I can learn and grow from the experience. I check myself to see where I might need more improvement. Sometimes I find the improvement should be along the lines of being more careful. Other times I find I must simply work on my patience, tolerance, or even forgiveness. While it is true that some people take advantage of others intentionally, some folks simply have not yet learned to behave in a manner that is conducive to the betterment of society at large. I receive many opportunities to learn from my mistakes, and these opportunities sometimes come in the form of being the victim of someone else's ploy. When I find someone has taken advantage of me, I can retaliate to get my revenge, or I can forgive, learn, and move on.

The principles I learn in my program also apply outside my program. We recommend to those in my program that we "practice these principles in all our affairs."

I used to love to talk about doing this. Actually, I still love to talk about it. The difference now is that I actually do it more often than I talk about it. My program teaches me principles for living, and when I practice them my life gets better.

I remember going to twelve-step meetings early in my recovery and talking about how to practice, outside my program, principles I have learned inside my program. I still go to many step meetings because I enjoy the opportunity to focus on the steps and to study them in greater depth. My favorite part of Step Twelve is "practicing the principles." When I was in these meetings, it seemed to me that everyone liked to focus on carrying the message to others, going on twelve-step calls, and having spiritual experiences. Since I have grown in my recovery I do notice more people talking about practicing the principles; I just didn't seem to notice it so much back then. I went on and on about practicing the principles and how important it is to do so "in all of our affairs." After having done this for a period of time—at more than a few twelve-step meetings—I was on my way home from a meeting, having just extolled this fact to all in attendance, when I realized that I didn't even know what the principles were. I knew they existed somewhere in the program—probably in the steps—yet I had no idea of what these principles might actually be. I couldn't list them to save my life. For a moment I felt like a fool; fortunately I turned this experience into a learning opportunity. I researched the principles. I discovered that there is indeed at least one principle guiding each of the Twelve Steps, and these principles show me what I should be practicing. The principles I've found to be most beneficial are acceptance, faith, surrender, trust, honesty, courage, willingness, humility, forgiveness, freedom, perseverance, patience, charity, and love. These principles are directly related to the steps and directly related to life.

I am learning to practice these principles in everyday life—in all my affairs. I do so to the best of my ability. While my ability to do so varies from day to day, I do my best to apply them wherever possible. It is easy to put these precepts to work during a meeting. For some reason, I know I need to be on my best behavior during a meeting. However, it becomes more difficult to behave in a consistently positive manner when I am dealing with the general public, when I am dealing with family and friends, and when I am dealing with everyday life. Practice within the safety of meetings allows me to apply my new behavior in a safe environment. The real test of my ability to change my behavior comes when I am not in the meetings.

The relationship between hearing "the message" and putting it to work in my life is a vivid example of the theme found in the story of the sermon, recounted earlier. If I hear something in a meeting and think, "That sounds wonderful," yet fail to put it to the test outside the confines of the meeting environment, I fail myself because I squander an opportunity to grow. But the opportunity is not lost forever, since failure is an opportunity to learn and grow. I do not have to throw away missed opportunities. Instead, I can commit myself to doing better next time. Recovery, like life, is a series of events. If at first you don't succeed, try, try, again. You never know where your efforts will lead.

What I learn in meetings—from my sponsor, from reading program literature, and from taking other actions the program suggests—quickly becomes a set of tools I can use in everyday life to make it better for myself and for those around me. The program mirrors life in order for me to learn new lessons with people who are trying to learn similar lessons. We can experiment on ourselves and on each other. We allow for mistakes and thereby encourage further growth. Once I feel I have sufficiently mastered a new behavior, attitude, thought process, or similar positive change, I can take it with me as I venture out into the real world. Each day I am a new person; each day I have new and exciting choices. It is my goal to make positive and healthy choices that will help me to become an even better person. This is my goal because I want to be happy, and I have found that being happy is a choice. It is far easier to choose to be happy when I am not all caught up in comparing myself with others.

When we are unhappy with ourselves, it is usually because we are preoccupied with comparing ourselves with others. "The grass is always greener" and "keeping up with the Joneses"—whoever they are—are expressions some use to refer to their tendency to compare themselves with others. This tendency to compare is not only not fun, it is unhealthy. The more time I spend comparing myself to others, the less time I have for positive change. The more time I spend on negative habits, the less time I have to practice positive changes in behavior. The more I practice comparing, the less progress I make toward becoming the person I really want to be. However, possibly the worst part of comparing myself to others is just how unfair I am to myself.

When I compare myself to someone else, it's like comparing apples to oranges—I'm comparing the way I feel against the way they appear. This cannot possibly be fair to either of us, but it is the only way I can compare myself without the other person's full participation. In order to compare myself to another person fairly, the other person must give me more information. We can have a foot race to compare our times, we can take out our checkbooks to compare finances, or we can talk about how we feel and what we think, then compare ourselves that way. Comparing the way I feel to the way someone else feels is the first step onto a slippery slope—covered in heavy grease—because I tend to compare my entire self to only a quick snapshot of how I see their life. I compare myself—my entire life, all my faults, and my low self-esteem—to what another person is experiencing over a short time frame. When I do this without their input, I can quickly gain downward momentum. This sick thinking is not part of my new normal.

Without the input of others, I have no idea what they think or feel; I only know what *I* think they think or feel. What ends up in my head is, without a doubt, what I think, and not what they may actually be thinking or feeling. It is this transference of my thoughts to them that is so harmful, yet I seem to do it without even a second thought. Substituting my thoughts for what another person may be thinking is one of the more insane things I do to myself.

Even if I do know what others are feeling, I must not become fixated upon a single moment of another person's life and compare my entire existence to it. That person has lived a life up until this moment, one filled with trials and tribulations, fun and excitement, ups and downs, just like mine. We are so alike, yet so very different. What I am actually witnessing is a snapshot of their existence; a mere fleeting moment. This moment will quickly become part of their past. If I compare myself to this snapshot and they seem to be something that I wish I were at that exact moment, then I have no place to go but down. Then again, if I am glad that I am not in their shoes, I have no place to go but up. I have found either direction of thought to be unhealthy for me. I am looking to avoid such self-guided trips on my mental roller coaster. The ride, while exhilarating if I am going up, usually leads me to feel bad about myself. Today I choose to feel good about myself. Freedom of choice is a wonderful thing. As long as I don't take a drink, I can continue to make healthy choices.

When I first came to my fellowship I was told to relate, and not compare. People who seemed to be happy, happier than I was, advised me that I would find it beneficial to center on the things I have in common with others, not our differences. I decided to listen, to learn, and to believe what I heard. I would not compare my using episodes with the way other people used. By refraining from doing so, I could relate to how they used, see how crazy it is to use like that, and then determine whether I had a problem myself. I was not there to determine if they had a problem; they were there to discover that for themselves.

First, I took a serious look at how comparing my old habits to those of others in the program hurt me; then I changed my way of thinking. By changing the way I thought, I was able to see my own problem and begin to do something about it. Since I like to take things a step or two farther than I should, I decided I would try, to the best of my ability, not to compare myself to others in the program. I decided it was not my concern if they were doctors or lawyers or members of any of the many professions where one can make lots of money. It didn't matter if they were down on their luck, out of work, or had little in the way of material possessions.

Eventually, I began to notice that many people had gone from one extreme to the other while in recovery. I heard people share their stories of "the before and after." I found that some people lost everything after they entered recovery. I heard others tell how they entered recovery, went back to school, got a good job, and began a new, prosperous life (monetarily speaking, of course). The stories that stuck with me the most were the ones wherein people told of how they had become happy, content, serene, and unflappable in the face of nearly everything I feared. I attached myself to these people. I wanted what they had, and I became willing to do what they had done in order to get it. I stopped comparing the differences and began relating to the similarities. Nearly anything that is possible for someone else is also possible for me. We are different, and we have differing physical, mental, emotional, and spiritual limitations. However, it is my job to find the things other people have that I feel would benefit me in some way. By learning these principles, then applying them to my life, I gain something, for myself and for the people who will ask me for help in the future. When they come to me, I will have more to offer them.

Practicing not comparing myself to others taught me that I must avoid making comparisons, whether in the program or in life. Now that I am in recovery, I can learn from almost anybody. I also discovered that it is important for me to pay attention to those I relate to outside the program. I spend much more time interacting with people outside the program than I do dealing with people in recovery. Therefore, I have found it nearly obligatory to carry with me the process of relating to others instead of comparing myself to others all the time. I simply do not learn by comparing the differences. I learn from relating, finding similarities, interacting, sharing, listening, dealing with people, and not withdrawing into my comparisons. I prefer not to hide between my inner world and the outside world of normal people just like me.

When I ask myself, "Am I different?" the answer is a resounding "yes." We all have differences; however, being different is a good thing. I learn through diversity if I am willing to pay attention. People who come from different walks of life have a wide variety of views on subjects I was able to see only from my perspective until I began to listen to them and to hear how they viewed the world. When I listen to others, without prejudging, I can learn many new things which can enhance my own life. I go to meetings to share my "experience, strength, and hope." I also go to meetings to benefit from others who share their stories. I want to know what other people do to make their lives better because I can apply this information to my own life to make it better. One of the greatest benefits of my program is the opportunity to learn.

In my program, I am a teacher once and a student many times. At every meeting I attend, I have the opportunity to teach once, yet I have many opportunities to learn. When I go to a meeting with twenty other people, if I share, I am a teacher for a brief moment. I spend the rest of the meeting as a student. There are twenty other people in the room—twenty other teachers. I have twenty opportunities to learn something new, and quite often, I learn many things. I learn from the diversity of the people. As they share their experiences with the group, they share their differing views of the world. Because of their diversity, I have the opportunity to pick up things I can use to grow in my existence, and to expand my knowledge base. Isn't that what life is all about—learning and growing? I attend meetings to be naturally and effortlessly happy while helping someone else or while learning and growing in my recovery.

Meetings are wonderful. I don't go to meetings just to go to meetings. I go to meetings to learn how to live life.

I can learn from the diversity of people everywhere. As I mentioned, I spend more time outside meetings than I do inside them. Why should I limit my opportunity to learn to time spent in meetings? If life is about learning, I have chances galore to learn. I can go to school, I can read books, join a book club to discuss the books I read, or attend seminars. I can live life. For me, meetings are more like a school classroom than real life. I learn in meetings, but I have little chance to actually practice what I've learned. I must forge ahead into the great unknown of life in order to truly practice and test what I have learned. As I practice new ideas, gain knowledge, and test a new behavior, I discover that one aspect of my life comes clearly into focus—becoming normal.

My desire to become normal and my new ability to live life as well as anybody else, including those who don't drink or use, necessitates that it is absolutely necessary to stop comparing myself to others who do drink and use and giving them some special credit for this ability. I cannot perform surgery, yet I am not jealous of the doctor who can. I do not consider a doctor to be more normal because he or she can do something I am unable to do. The same is true for many things in life. I am not much of an athlete or mechanic; I don't do crafts or knit sweaters. It would be a waste of time for me to list the things I do not do well, or for which I have no capacity. Drinking is among the things I do not do well. Because of this fact, I choose not to drink. Like many things I tried—only to discover I lacked ability—I have quit trying to drink successfully. I tried playing the guitar, found I had little talent for it, and gave it up. I still like to listen to music but accept that I cannot play the guitar. Why should I begrudge those who drink, or stay away from a party simply because others drink? I would not avoid the party because there was music (even live music) and I was unable to play an instrument. Worse yet, why should I give someone else a higher stature than I am willing to give myself, simply because they do not suffer the horrible consequences from drinking that I do? This is, by far, the worst comparison I can make. It's not their fault that I cannot play a musical instrument or that I cannot drink safely. I choose not to play the guitar and I choose not to drink.

When I compare myself to those who can drink socially, referring to them as normal, I am saying to myself and to others that I am not normal. If I, even subconsciously, believe they are normal because they can drink socially, I am telling myself that I will never be normal and that I will never have a good life. Because my drinking is abnormal, I allow it to become a limitation that could potentially ruin my life. I must end this unhealthy comparison. I must let others be who they are while I allow myself to be who I am. We all have limitations. Even those who can drink successfully have a long list of things they can never do. Why should I get caught up in the fact that they can drink? It is a waste of my time and happiness. It doesn't bother me if they drink; it only bothers me if I drink, so why make such a comparison? If I want to do so, why not make a comparison that is more beneficial? Why not compare my disease to another disease?

As far as diseases go, I am very lucky.

While addiction is the only disease I know of in which the person with the disease is blamed for having it, I have come to see the reasoning behind the blaming.

People used to blame me for having this disease because they simply could not understand why I would allow this illness to ruin my life, when I have at my disposal the tools to put it into remission. My behavior mystified them. They did not understand my insane desire to maintain my illness through my own actions when I had the power to choose and to end the suffering. They didn't understand the malady any more than I did. However, they did know something I didn't know. I do have a degree of control over the course of my illness that those with other diseases do not have. I must participate in my disease for it to persevere. I continued to feed my disease for a very long time. Eventually, I decided that "enough was enough."

I have heard in many meetings the comparison between addicts and people with cancer. It was suggested that if presented with a simple set of suggestions—like those laid out in program literature—and the promise that they would become cancer-free if they followed these simple suggestions, cancer patients would accept such a cure with open arms. This is understandable, because they know they are sick, while an addict often cannot see the illness within. Since treatments differ from illness to illness, we can't offer cancer patients the cure that works for addiction; it just won't work for what ails them. However, this "cure" will work for those who suffer from addiction.

A person today usually has many treatment options when diagnosed with cancer. These usually include chemotherapy, surgery, and rehabilitation. Their doctor may also prescribe them medication, give them advice on changing their diet, and offer some new habits in order to treat their condition. The doctor also will tell the patient what their odds are of having a relapse. The treatment for addiction does not work the same way.

Those with the disease of addiction are usually presented with very different options. Available options may come from friends, family, or even a doctor. These options usually include—but most likely are not limited to—simply laying off the "stuff," cutting down on drinking, or going to rehab. They can also choose to join a recovery group like mine. If the patient agrees that he or she has a problem (which doesn't seem to be an issue with a cancer patient), he or she might seek help. An addict presented with these options might choose rehab (treatment). During the treatment program, a doctor will most likely give the patient advice on diet. Stopping drinking was a significant change in my diet, as was starting to eat properly. Like the cancer doctor, the addiction-treatment professionals can provide patients with medication and offer some new habits in order to treat their conditions. The medication may be anything from short-term treatment for withdrawal symptoms to attending meetings. The new habits might include such things as drinking only liquids that do not contain alcohol, eating properly, getting some exercise, and attending meetings. Everyone I knew wanted me to go to meetings—even the people at the meetings told me to "keep coming back." It is one suggestion I found very beneficial. I figured that my best thinking got me where I was, and that if I gave my program a chance, my life had to improve.

The doctor, treatment facilitator, or even other program members will divulge to the "patient" the odds of having a relapse. Here is where I am very lucky compared to the cancer patient. We have both had to change many things in our lives: our diets, our habits, our medication, the places we go, and the people we see. Our treatment process touches everything we do. However, cancer patients have no guarantee that their disease will not come back.

And while it's true that addicts have no guarantee that they will not relapse, I know today that if I "take my medicine" properly, I will not relapse. The cancer patients have no such luck. They can do everything right—take their medicine, eat right, change habits, you name it—and the cancer can still come back—without their consent. Being an addict, if I do everything I am supposed to do, I do not need to get loaded. The most important thing I can do is to not pick up, and my disease will not become active again. I must follow the plan of recovery laid out before me. For my disease to return I must participate in the process by taking a drink or using a drug. Any kind of mood- or mind-altering substance will do.

I have never heard of anyone getting out of bed, saying their prayers, calling their sponsor, going to a meeting, and not drinking or drugging, and winding up loaded. It just doesn't happen. I have come to believe relapse does not happen if I do what I am supposed to do. In fact, the word "relapse" means something different to me than it generally does to most twelve-step program members I know. Relapse, as I define it, is to fall back into a former state, especially after apparent improvement—through no fault of the person with the illness. Take the example of someone with the flu. He seems to feel better and is advised by his doctor to stay home and rest for a few more days, and yet he returns to his regular daily activities too soon. I don't consider it a relapse when he again gets sick. He didn't know for sure that he would become ill again if he went about his regular routine a day or two early, or as soon as he felt up to it. Surely, there was a chance he might not have become sick again. As an addict, there is a difference for me: I have a one-hundred-percent chance of returning to illness if I drink. There are no ifs, no ands, no buts, no rationalizations, no justifications, and no excuses for putting the bottle to my mouth while thinking, "This won't make me sick."

It happens, though. I have done it myself. I just didn't call it a relapse, and to this day, I will not call it a relapse. I say, "I got drunk again." I say this because it is the truth. I chose to drink. I can have a million excuses, reasons, justifications, and rationalizations. In fact, I did so at the time. I only saw the truth in retrospect. The truth is that I knew it would make me sick again. Either that or I didn't believe I was an addict. For me the answer was simple. I did not believe I was sick, or if you prefer, I wished things were different. I wished I weren't an addict. Today I know I am—I know that to drink or drug is to become sick again.

I have a choice in my return to illness. The cancer patients do not have this choice. They can follow all suggestions and still their cancer can recur. When I make comparisons such as these, it makes it easier for me to take my medication. My "medication" consists of going to meetings, calling my sponsor, reading approved literature, and, most of all, keeping drugs and alcohol from entering my body. Unfortunately, my brain likes to work against me at times. I learned I have a built-in "forgetter," that I have a disease that tells me I am not sick, and that I have a thinking problem. My first sponsor told me there are no problems, only opportunities. Today I have the opportunity to look at the problem of thinking as it relates to the problem of my addiction.

MY THINKING IS MY OWN.

THERE IS NO ESCAPE FROM IT.

YET I RAN AS FAST AS I COULD

FROM MY OWN THINKING,

OR AT LEAST FROM TAKING

RESPONSIBILITY FOR IT.

I LOOKED TO OTHER PEOPLE

FOR TOO MUCH INPUT,

TOO MUCH HELP, AND

TOO MUCH APPROVAL.

4
THINKING

I've learned I have a thinking problem and that my disease centers on my thought process. Actually, what I have learned is that my disease is twofold. The thinking problem has allied with an allergy to create a formidable adversary. My faulty reasoning tells me that I can have "just one"; however, that "one" kicks my allergy into action and I can't stop. Therefore, I have concluded that when it comes to my disease, I do not have so much a using problem as a stopping problem. I have decided to focus on the thinking portion of the problem. If I can clear this up, I stand a much better chance of not having to worry about the stopping problem. I will know better than to start in the first place. I will take the actions necessary to prevent the reemergence of the allergy.

When I first got into recovery, I thought that if I had a thinking problem, then I had to determine what the problem was, where it came from, how I got it, who gave it to me, and even why it happened to me. I used to believe I needed to analyze everything—figure out the hows and whys of whatever was wrong with my life.

In the beginning, this was also how I approached working the steps; as I worked Step Six for the first time (being "entirely ready" to have my Higher Power remove all the defects of character that prevented me from being of service to Him), I thought, "I'd better know exactly what these defects are." (Of course, they had emerged when I did my fourth and fifth steps.) However, I came to realize that I did not need to know exactly which defects needed to be removed, or where they originated. (In fact, many traits I had originally thought were defects turned out not to be.) I had to let my Higher Power determine which character traits were defects, and which needed to be removed; all I had to do to work the step was to be willing. I didn't need to overanalyze the defects in detail in order to have them removed.

Similarly, I realized I didn't need to analyze my "thinking problem" in relation to my active addiction. I realized that I did not need to know exactly what was wrong in order to begin making corrections.

I must admit, the desire to know for sure is very seductive: If I have a thinking problem, where did it come from? How did my thinking get broken? I wanted to know whether I was born that way. I "thought myself" into believing that I had learned to think improperly; that I had somehow broken a perfectly good mind. There must have been something tangible—something identifiable— that had led me to the breaking point. I sat in deep contemplation, trying to pinpoint exactly what had gone wrong, how I had ventured down the wrong path. It took time, but I finally discovered what I was trying to do. I was trying to find a way to blame others for my plight.

While searching for a possible cause of my thinking problem, I came across the following potential answer. What I was really doing was using faulty thinking to fix faulty thinking. These days, I tend to believe this method will not work. The example below led me to some very important ideas about how to continue moving forward in my personal growth.

When I was very young, too young to even know what was going on in life, so young that the boxes were more important than the presents themselves, I was told that Santa Claus brought me gifts every year at Christmas. The Easter Bunny brought me candy at Easter. As soon as I was old enough for my baby teeth to start falling out, the Tooth Fairy paid me cash for each tooth I put under my pillow. It wasn't long after I started receiving these payments that I found out Santa Claus and the Easter Bunny did not really exist. There was still some insistence that the Tooth Fairy was the one paying for my teeth. I have a younger sister, so I was expected to "continue to believe" in Santa and the Easter Bunny even though I knew better. My family expected me to perpetuate the lies "for her sake."

I felt that these lies were innocent when I initially thought about them. I decided that since they came from the people I depended upon for my food, clothing, and shelter, they had not been very damaging to me. Most of the love I received came from these people, as did my sense of belonging and my safety and security, as well as my self-esteem. They were the people who checked under my bed to make sure there were no monsters to get me during the night. They were the same people who patched up my knee when I fell off my tricycle and kissed my invisible boo-boos to make them better. They baked me cookies and made me cakes and gave me presents for my birthday. These very people told me not to lie. When my brother and I fought and my parents asked us what had happened, honesty on our part was always expected. When I broke a plate, they demanded to know who did it. They expected the truth. Yet they were lying to me, or at least warping my understanding of the truth.

My parents told me about God. Since they were Christian, they told me about Jesus. I could not see, feel, hear, taste, or touch this God. Yet I was expected to "have faith" and believe that this entity existed. It was difficult, but I continued to believe. The God my parents told me about could also turn against me. My parents told me that if I didn't behave—I was a very mischievous child—God would strike me down, or punish me. Today, I know a much different God. But in the early years, even though I wanted to believe in God, He frightened me. If I did believe, He might strike me down if I was bad. He might do so even if I didn't believe. Something was terribly wrong with this concept of God. I felt confused. I did not know what to think.

It is no wonder I was confused. The people I loved most had lied to me, while at the same time telling me not to lie. They had lied about three fictitious characters, Santa Claus, the Easter Bunny, and the Tooth Fairy, only to tell me later that they did not exist. During this time, they taught me to believe in God and then turned Him against me. It's no wonder my "thinker is broken." It's no wonder growing up was so difficult. It's no wonder that when I was old enough to discover the magic of alcohol and the way it helped me to not think about all of this stuff, I used it improperly.

I discovered that on many occasions I was to look to others for my self-worth. Right or wrong, my parents taught me that what others thought of me was important—too important. In fact, I learned that what others thought of me was more important than what I thought of myself. This was another lie I believed. I came to understand that this lie wasn't necessarily told to me; rather, I had learned it through observation. I automatically accepted this way of thinking as normal because I had no way of knowing it was a lie.

Through no fault of their own, my parents raised me to seek their approval. They told me when I was a good boy or a bad boy. Of course, I wanted to be a good boy, so I tried to do the things they told me were good. They told me what was good because I did not know good from bad. In most cases, I think they were correct in the things they taught me about good and bad, right and wrong. They told me things like "Don't touch the stove" because I would get burned, not to throw stones because people could get hurt or things could get broken, and not to fight because there were better ways to resolve conflicts. They also told me to pay attention in school, to learn, get a diploma, go on to college and obtain a degree, find a good job to support myself. Most of the things they taught me were useful and correct. However, I did not always pay attention or heed the advice I was given. I can understand the wisdom in their actions. Still, I continued to look for reasons why my thinker seemed to be "broken."

Unfortunately, what they also taught me—what I believe I learned from them—was that I had to rely on them for basic needs and for their approval. By extension, they taught me to look to others outside the family for approval, and they did this by forcing me to seek their approval in nearly everything I did. I had to ask if I could go to my friend's house or stay up late, have a snack before dinner, or wear certain clothes. If I did not follow their guidelines, they punished me. I did my best to stay within their guidelines and always sought their approval. Sometimes the approval was not enough; the attention was lacking, and I would seek more attention by doing things I knew were bad, knowing I would end up in trouble. Still, in doing bad things I would obtain the attention I needed.

My mother told me recently that when I was younger I used to ask myself a maximum of two questions before doing something I knew to be wrong. The first question was: "Will I get caught?" If I thought I could get away with whatever the illicit activity was, there was no need to ask the second question. However, if I thought that I might have gotten caught, I would ask myself: "Will it be worth the punishment if I do get caught?" If I thought the activity would be worth the punishment I was almost certain to receive, I would participate in the tomfoolery. I believe I did this as a way to push boundaries and to assert my independence. Although I no longer view this process as a healthy way to accomplish the task, it seemed proper at the time. Still, this was my way of seeking approval, because seeking attention is really a form of approval seeking. Of course, I did not perform these acts until later in my youth.

I went to school—as do most children in America— and the approval seeking I practiced was reinforced immediately. From my first day in kindergarten, I learned that I had to obey the teacher. I had to act a certain way, do certain things, and obey certain rules. I learned when to take a nap, not to eat the glue, and to share with the other children. If I did what they told me, I was a good boy. If I did not comply, I was labeled a troublemaker and punished.

I learned, through this constant reinforcement, to seek the approval of the teacher and even of the other students, who might tell on me if I did not behave. I learned that what these other people thought of me was extremely important. I had to conform. I could not just be myself—that might not be right—I had to adapt, change, and try to fit in. I didn't want to change, or I didn't think I could.

Through this process, which continued throughout high school, I learned that I should not be myself, no matter how badly I wanted to assert my independence. I learned that I needed the approval of others. I grew older and entered high school, and my approval seeking evolved. If I wanted to play football, I had to fit in with the jocks, who shunned the nerds. If I wanted to be in the band, I was a nerd. If I acted in a play, I would certainly meet with the disapproval of those I ran with. These were unwritten rules. However, almost everyone understood and conformed to them. Anyone who did not conform was mercilessly ridiculed. Fear of ridicule helped keep the rest of us in line. This constant pressure was present long before high school.

By the time I was in sixth grade I figured out that I was an approval seeker. I just did not realize how detrimental it could be to my personal growth. When I was eleven, my music teacher told me that I had a wonderful voice and should consider singing as a career. Having a warped sense of approval seeking, I wondered what he wanted from me. What did he stand to gain from my going into music? If I chose a musical career, how would he benefit? I was trying to figure out how I would please him by living my life in the way he had suggested. It never occurred to me that someone might do something to help me without expecting something in return.

In the long run I did not follow through on the musical career. By the time I got to high school, I was already taking ballet and jazz dancing, which was way out of the ordinary for a guy at the time. I figured that if I sang, that would be a bit too much. Although my close friends knew the truth, some of the people who knew I was studying ballet already thought I was gay, and I didn't like their disapproval. I decided that if I sang and acted, even more people would disapprove of me. Deep down inside I knew I would never be popular enough not to worry about alienating others in order to be myself. I did not dare cause more disapproval. Therefore, I did not sing, I did not act, and I did not do many of the things I enjoyed. I was not myself because other people would not approve of who I wanted to be.

Instead, I played football my freshman year. I was four-foot-ten and lightweight enough to wrestle in the ninety-eight-pound class when the football season ended. I was too small for football, but I played that year anyway. I was fourth-string everything and I sat on the bench. I never played football again. I did wrestle my freshman year and I did quite well. However, the varsity coach made it blatantly clear I would have no place on the varsity team because there was another guy in my weight class who was already a varsity champion in his freshman year. More disapproval meant no more wrestling. Still, I continued with sports because I was afraid of the crushing disapproval I might encounter if I attempted to sing, dance, and act in plays like I wanted. My next sport was baseball, where I was cut from the team my sophomore year because I did not play my freshman year. Crazy as it sounds, that was the reason they gave for cutting me from the team. I did not play the previous year, so I could not play the next year. In my junior year, hockey came to my school. I tried out for the team. I had been playing hockey in pick-up games for a few years and had been skating since my parents bought me a pair of double-bladed skates when I was five years old. I was desperate for approval, and I figured I had a good chance to make the team. I didn't make it. I was the last guy cut. However, the coach told me I had a lot of potential. I asked if I could be the team manager, get some ice time, and improve my game in order to make the team in my senior year. I did become the team manager, went to every practice, and improved enough that I thought making the team would be a cinch the following year.

At the time I became manager of the hockey team, I had nothing else to draw from for approval. I had exhausted all other sports, acting, singing, and dancing, and had been ruled "out of my mind" long before I reached this point. My grades were too low to get on the debate team, the chess team, or any other team that required "brain power." Hockey appeared to be my last chance to gain the approval I desperately needed. Becoming manager of the hockey team allowed me to go to every practice. I participated in scrimmages, suited up, played when I was allowed, and improved my game tremendously. I tried out one last time during my senior year, and was cut from the team. I had met complete and total disapproval, and my self-esteem reached a new all-time low.

When I figured out that this was how my thinking had become "broken," my next immediate thought was that I had a wonderful excuse for the person I had become because of all of these "tragedies" in my life. Directly on the heels of that thought was the fact that I had created an excuse. I wasn't looking for an excuse. I didn't want— or didn't think I wanted—any excuses. I was looking for answers and sought some truth—truth about myself. In fact, I had been looking for mistakes I had made, not to blame other people. I thought of ways to relieve others of their part in my problems—but because my thinker was broken, there was no way I was going to blame anyone but myself for the turn my life had taken.

The search for answers continued. I told myself that none of what happened should be used as an excuse for my becoming an addict. I chose to use the way I did—to kill the crazy in me—whether it was through faulty thinking, allergy, or by making poor choices. I repeated to myself, "I'm not making excuses." I'm doing my best, now that I am in recovery, to figure out why I used the way I used. Even though I am quite certain I will never be able to answer this question, I somehow cannot seem to stop searching for answers. How crazy does this sound? I am looking for something I know I will never find. Still, I wanted desperately to know why I did the things I did. At first, I thought finding the "why" would release me from my responsibilities, or at least explain why I should live up to them. Living up to my responsibilities is a lot more work than being released from them. I believe I was looking for release. Although I told myself at the time that I was looking for self-improvement, I can see in retrospect that I was searching for a scapegoat. It is hard to figure out exactly what I was doing. Even when I am convinced that my intentions are proper, I can still go astray. The results are often improper actions that leave me baffled as to what went wrong.

For me, there is often a "fine line" between searching for the truth and looking for excuses. Often the fine line is obscure, and not easily found. The fine line does not appear until I have something concrete in my hand—something

I can call the truth. However, once I have this new piece of information, look out, because that is when the fine line emerges and the finger pointing begins. The fine line says, "That's why you did it" or "You can cross over me now." I want to believe that it is far easier to blame others for my actions than to take responsibility for them. Since I used to live on the other side of the fine line, my code of ethics was "I didn't do it." It is all too easy to slip back into the behavior of blaming others for my actions. It is time to stop blaming others and to take responsibility. I am through blaming others. I am simply looking for the truth. I was still telling myself this even though I had no idea what I would do with this truth if and when I found it. I went on "making no excuses," or telling myself that I was making none.

Besides, how could I blame my parents, grandparents, aunts, and uncles for telling me there is a Santa? Nearly every family does it. My parents raised me as other parents raise their children. In fact, my parents raised me as they were raised by their parents. I would be crazy to blame my parents for the way they raised me and for my drinking. I might as well point my finger all the way back to Adam and Eve or the amoeba, if you are an evolutionist. It is not about blame anymore. Instead, it is about healing, recovery, living, changing, growing, and loving. My denial was alive and well as I continued looking for excuses.

Many people have lived through much worse than I have, and they have never abused substances or engaged in addictive behaviors in order to cope. They somehow found a way to deal with more difficult situations than I ever had to deal with in a manner that proved to be more positive. My issues must belong to me. Even if I look at others who lived through my exact situation—the same environment—

there is no excuse. After all, my brother and sister are not addicts. We all grew up in the same home with the same parents, had very similar opportunities, and were loved equally, treated equally, and asked to produce equally. They didn't use over it. Therefore, while I am tempted to look deeper into the causes of my problems, I must look deeper into myself for answers and be careful not to point fingers at others. Others do not do my thinking for me. Even if I abdicate my responsibility for my thinking to others, the final decisions are mine to make, and I must make them whether I like it or not. My thinking is my own. There is no escape from it. Yet I ran as fast as I could from my own thinking, or at least from taking responsibility for it. I looked to other people for too much input, too much help, and too much approval. I was beginning to make up some ground here, especially when I began to wonder about a few things.

Who was I trying to convince with my tirade about not making excuses? Other people? My parents? Was it someone else? The answer is absolutely not. I was trying to convince myself. I discovered the truth: that I had been looking for excuses for my old drinking behavior for so long that I could not stop looking, even after I had been in recovery for a while. Even after I had worked through many of the Twelve Steps with a wonderful sponsor, I was still looking for excuses.

Maybe this is because the difference between excuses and reasons is so slim. I have come to believe that reasons are things I have little or no control over—situations where I have no real choice in the matter—while excuses are more or less concocted. I cannot go to the party because I am going to the football game. Here I have chosen the football game over the party. I make these choices all the time, yet

I am often unaware I am offering excuses because I think going to the football game is a good reason to miss the party. My newfound logic would lead me to believe that a reason is a choice I have no control over. Another example is that I am on my way to meet my friend at an appointed time in order to get to the football game before kickoff. I have a flat tire on my car, which requires time to change and causes me to be late for our meeting. Some might argue that I should have given myself more time to drive to the meeting. However, I have a flat tire so infrequently that it seems a bit excessive to expect it to happen, and to leave early enough to allow time to change a flat tire. In this instance, I have a reason for being late. I did not choose to have a flat. My real difficulty with excuses and reasons is the way I can turn an excuse into a reason without consciously thinking about it. I have to look carefully to see if I had a choice in the matter. If I did, it is an excuse. If I did not, it is a reason. The difference is so fine that it can be difficult to see.

If I am no longer looking for a release from my responsibilities, and if I am truly willing to accept the fact that I am responsible for my actions, then I must be able to stop making excuses. I must accept who I am and how I got here. I must acknowledge that I made choices in my past that led me to become who I am today. I must do this because the simple truth is that it no longer matters to me how I got here. It only matters that I am here. It does not matter how my thinker became broken, only that it needs fixing. I had to forget about my childhood if it involved blame. I had to learn to deal with life on life's terms. I must live in today, not the past, and not the future. Finally, I made some progress.

My exercise was not entirely futile. It helped me to see some things I had previously avoided or overlooked. By looking into my past, I discovered the part I played. By trying to look at what I was dealing with, I discovered what I had been avoiding: my part in the greater scheme. The trip through the past was fraught with pitfalls. I fell into many of them. However, in the process, I was learning. It took me quite a while to figure out these things.

All the crazy decisions I made—to be different from what I wanted to be—were based solely on things I did not even know existed within me, such as fear and selfishness. I wanted what I wanted when I wanted it, and I didn't care who had to pay for it. Because of this, I lived in constant fear of discovery and of being labeled as a fraud. I would do things I did not want to do in order to get other people to do the things I wanted them to do for me. I cannot pinpoint when this behavior began. I only know that at some point it took over my life and my sense of being. Since my fellowship taught me that my biggest problems were fear, selfishness, and resentment, I finally discovered the truth. I thought it was safe for me to take another trip into my past to see if I could determine just when my selfishness began. I was not able to nail down an exact time frame because my past is fraught with selfish acts. The earliest selfish act I can remember shows me that my thinking was more concerned with getting things than with how I could contribute to the lives of others.

When I was five years old, my dad and I were in a Sears Surplus store where they sold farming equipment. We were walking down the aisle, and sitting right in the middle of this aisle was a three-bottom plow. My dad pointed at the plow and asked me if I wanted one. I replied with excitement, "Yeah, yeah! What is it?" I did not even know what it was, but I knew I wanted it. I was selfish enough at age five that I did not care if I had any use for the item; I simply wanted it. I acted this way about almost everything. I did so to the point where, if I wanted something enough, I would manipulate people into providing it for me. Since I was selfish and manipulative, I believed others were too. I now understand why I thought my sixth grade music teacher had an ulterior motive when he suggested that I pursue a singing career.

I believed others acted the same way I would under similar circumstances. If I was a liar, other people lied. If I stole, I had to be on the lookout for thieves. If I had ulterior motives, so did other people. Since I was selfish, other people had to be selfish—they must have been looking for what they could get from me. This negative thinking (and negative living) had to, and did, change.

This thinking—that everyone wanted something from me—led to fear, and a self-imposed pressure that was nerve-wracking, to say the least. Since it was self-imposed, it never let up. Since I did not realize I was the cause, I did not know I could change this behavior. Instead, my distorted view of reality did not allow for any measure of "insightful thinking." I lived under the pressure, doing my best to get what I wanted, without regard for the feelings of others. At the same time, I sought approval. This is a brutal cycle of dysfunction. I beat myself up for many years because it did not occur to me that my turmoil was self-inflicted and self-perpetuating. While it was excruciatingly uncomfortable, this behavior felt like an old glove; it fit me too well for me to abandon the discomfort. In fact, I wasn't even aware I could let go of the pain and that I could change the way I acted and reacted to others and to life's challenges.

No matter how much I hated the way I was, I thought I would never change. Change was impossible, or at least too difficult for me to attempt. Until I drank myself to the depths of despair and reached a level of discomfort I could no longer bear, I was unwilling to consider the possibility of change. I could not bring myself to take even the smallest steps. I did nothing until my life became so desperate that something had to change or else I would end up dying a miserable, lonely death. Like any addict, I followed one path until there were only two alternatives, one undesirable and the other insufferable. Life had become black and white, and I could not see the shades of gray. I followed my drinking, fear, resentment, and selfishness until I reached a terrible fork in the road or, as some say, the jumping-off point—people in recovery programs know this place and this state of mind very well. It is that point at which the alcoholic or addict can no longer live with the pain, and there seems to be no third option. I reached this impasse in large part by looking to others for approval, while at the same time doing everything in my power to manipulate and alienate these same people. I felt as though I was hopeless, yet my problems were largely of my own doing. I could not see myself for who I was.

Regardless of how I reached the position in which I found myself, I discovered that I did want to change. I just wasn't sure how to go about it. I first quit doing drugs and I managed to quit drinking, which was something I had been certain would never happen as I neared the end of my drinking days. While not drinking was enough for me at first, it was not long before I was looking for more. Some call the first weeks or months of happiness that follow the cessation of alcohol abuse as a "pink cloud." Call it what you will. I soon discovered, "this too shall pass." I surfed on my pink cloud for some time, but when the wave of happiness I found in recovery reached the sandy shores of reality, I had nothing with which to protect myself from the sudden jolt. Using was no longer an option. I wanted to stay sober, yet I had no real knowledge of how to deal with life without using.

What I discovered upon my arrival in reality was that I did not want to stay in recovery. However, I really did not want to get loaded. I didn't want to stay in recovery, because I did not know how; I had little idea of how life worked because I had spent my entire life avoiding the learning process. Still, I did not want to get high because I knew what that would mean. I had tasted happiness (whether it was a pink cloud or not), and I wanted more. I talked with my sponsor, who said that real happiness could be found as long as I did not drink or use. He also mentioned there was a lot of life to deal with as well. Life, he told me, was a combination of enjoyment and pain. While some emotional experiences are stronger than others, all are necessary and none will kill me, unlike drugs and alcohol. "This too shall pass" would have to become my motto if I was to make progress, he told me, and progress would carry its own toll. How I approach paying the price of progress is up to me. I know that now, and I am sure I did not fully understand it then. So much of my life is up to me now that I am sober, and how I deal with life has much to do with my attitude. I had to change my thinking to change my attitude, but how do I change something that has haunted me my whole life?

I have heard many people say, while pointing at their heads, "This is a bad neighborhood and I can't go up here alone." I believed this for a very long time, too long perhaps. At some point I realized that, just like using or not using seemed a terrible choice, going into the neighborhood of my mind was really something I had to do. Just like when I had to quit using or suffer intolerable consequences, I had to learn to change my thinking or live a life of prolonged suffering, whether I picked up again or not. If my mind was a bad neighborhood, I had to clean it up.

Not long into my recovery, I bought a house. While I like to think I live in a good part of town, if I discovered the neighborhood I lived in was a bad place to live, I could sell my house and move. When it comes to my head, moving is not an option. Since I could come up with no other alternative, I concluded that cleaning up the neighborhood of my mind was the only option available. I came to this conclusion begrudgingly; I did not like the idea of cleaning up a place that I was terrified to inhabit. However, I was convinced that the idea of inhabiting a terrifying place was intensely undesirable. There was no other choice; it had to be done.

I could live in a despicable mind, mired in my own thinking, dragged through life against my will, or roll up my sleeves and do what appeared to be highly undesirable work. This seemed my only option. Hiring others to do the work was impossible. I discovered there was help available—there always is, especially in my program—but I could tap this resource for consultation purposes only; the work was mine to do. There are no contractors for the mind. It is an "inside job." I felt up to the task. At first I resented the idea that I should be required to go to so much effort, and I soon realized that resentment is not my ally, but my foe. Eventually I came to accept the fact that I would have to do the work. Regrettably, I did not know what would be required. How could I change my thinking process? I consulted my trusted friends in the program, I talked to my sponsor, and I prayed. Finally an answer came.

How we think and talk has a tremendous effect upon how we perceive reality and how we live our lives. I had a very poor understanding of what life is all about. This lack of knowledge seems to be common among alcoholics. Although my past thinking was misguided, I knew I could change it. A well-known prayer led me to this conclusion. All I need is the courage to change the things I can—in this case, my thinking. I was in need of courage and a plan. Believing that I already had a plan, I sought the necessary courage. To summon the courage, I decided I needed to convince myself that it would be worth the effort. This sounded easy enough. If something is worth the effort, I will do it; I have done so my entire life. Even during the darkest days of what appeared to be my worst drinking, I was still willing to change my actions in order to do the things I considered worth the effort. Changing my thinking was a different beast altogether. If I changed my thinking, I could most certainly become a new person. I would become inexperienced at being me. The fear was paralyzing. I had to start slowly. Again, I consulted my trusted friends in the program. I talked to my sponsor and I prayed. Gradually, answers began to reveal themselves. As I began paying more attention to the changes in my thinking and my life, the answers magically appeared.

One of my first discoveries was that all conscious action requires thought. I tried to change my thinking, and even that required thought. In the process of changing my thoughts, I realized that everything I do requires some thought. I thought about getting out of bed in the morning before my feet hit the floor. Sure, my body moves without much thought on my part, but there is still a thought process taking place as my feet hit the floor. Most of the time, I am thinking about other things as I go about my morning routine. I may be thinking about the day ahead, work I must do, or the fun I will have. If I am lucky, even my work is fun. If it isn't, I can change that, too.

The truth I realized about my thinking is that I do it all the time. When I am awake, I am thinking. Even when I sleep, I dream, which is another form of thinking. Sometimes my brain is on autopilot, and thoughts just come and go. At other times, I am deep in thought. Quite often, I am thinking on multiple levels at the same time. Thinking should not scare me. I should be used to it by now. Suddenly the idea hit me: "I'm afraid not so much of thinking, but of what I think." I have some pretty scary thoughts—they seem to come along all too often. Some just appear out of nowhere. Horrible thoughts, crazy thoughts, these thoughts are the kind I feared. Then one day I came across a quote by St. Francis of Assisi and it had to do with thoughts that arise during meditation, but it seemed to me that it could apply to any unwanted or intrusive thoughts. We may notice birds as they fly overhead, he said, but we don't let them roost in our hair. I pondered this quote and its meaning for several days. I soon realized that the thoughts that fly into my head do not make me who I am. I don't even have to give them the space to roost. The thought does not make the man, the action does.

Thoughts had been running my life, when action should have been. Sure, I have to think in order to act, but I do not have to act just because I think. Many times I have violent thoughts—like the ones provoked by other drivers who pull out in front of me in traffic. But I don't act on them. Crazy thoughts come and go, and not just with alcoholics. I have talked with many people who seem to have no need for a recovery program. They all tell me they have similar thoughts. They tell me that since thoughts come and go, the key is to let them go. What a concept. I must take responsibility for my actions, but my thoughts can stay with me, or I can let them go and no consequences will happen. Consequences require an action. I have found that the thoughts I allow to stay with me are the ones upon which I will eventually act. Therefore, the functional thing to do is to let negative thoughts go. This led me to yet another revelation.

My thoughts are my choices. I put this to the test and found it to be correct. I decided to take action with regard to my thought process. I discovered that actually choosing my thoughts required a process, so it seems I found yet another process in life. In order to choose my thoughts, I had to watch what I was thinking about throughout the day in order to know what kind of choices were available. That was only the beginning of my renewed understanding that my thoughts were my choice.

How many times have you heard someone say, "Watch what you are doing"? How many times has this statement been directed at you? I cannot count the number of times I have been scolded in this manner. However, I have not heard it directed at me since I began watching my thinking. I am an extremist at times and I tend to swing the pendulum all the way in one direction. I do it without thinking, and quite often it is not the way I intended. I thought, why not try it on purpose? Instead of "Watch what you are doing," I changed it to "Watch what you are thinking." I applied it to myself because I wanted to change my thinking process, and trying to apply things to other people never seemed to work. If I watched what I was thinking, what I was doing would take care of itself.

I began to think of my mind as a sort of "nightclub" (although one where no booze was served!), with the entire cast of characters any such business would contain. There were patrons (thoughts), bouncers (guardians of order), and upper management. This last group oversaw everything that went on from their "upstairs office." Any patron who got out of line would be taken care of, first by the bouncers, and then, if necessary, by upper management! And presiding over it all, of course, was me! I had ultimate responsibility; I was the "club owner," so to speak.

Since the bouncers weren't trained initially, it was the club owner's job to oversee their work to ensure they operated effectively. (The real work always came back to me.) I supervised the bouncers. Maybe it would be more correct to say I watched my thoughts through the eyes of the bouncers. When a patron (thought) wanted access, a bouncer checked it at the door. The bouncer would then inform the club owner (me) about the thought in order to find out what to do with it. After careful evaluation, I would tell him what to do with that particular thought. Soon, the bouncers were able to do their work with less direct supervision from the club owner! Even though this safeguard was an imaginary setup—one that admittedly sounds a little weird—it helped me in two very important ways.

The first thing this new process did was to slow my thinking. I had to treat every thought separately. This brought my thoughts-per-second ratio way down. Every improbable or dubious thought had to be dealt with, no matter how minor it seemed. For example, while scratching my nose did not become a burden to my thought process, I did begin to notice the procedure my brain went through in order to make the action a reality. I was afraid, at least at first, that this might bring my thinking to a standstill. Giving passing thoughts the status of full cogitation might bring the entire system to a screeching halt. But my fears about this were unfounded, as usual. By monitoring my thought process, I slowed it down. Thoughts that used to scurry about in my head like children on a playground; running here and there, creating havoc without doing anything productive, were slowed to a walk. With the rules change, and the introduction of the "nightclub system," my thoughts had to prove they were worthy of taking up valuable space in my head.

The second advantage of having bouncers was that they relieved some of the stress that came from having to do all the work myself. When a thought popped into my head, it would come into contact with a bouncer. While the bouncer was imaginary, so was the thought! The imaginary bouncer informed me of the imaginary thought and whether its intentions were honorable. I could decide what I wanted to do about it, then turn the rest of the job back over to the bouncer. If a negative thought came cruising by, looking for a fun place to hang out, I could inform the bouncer to tell the thought to go away. Of course, I did the actual telling, but the imaginary bouncer created a kind of "buffer zone." Some thoughts were persistent, especially in the beginning when I was still new and inexperienced at this thinking revolution.

Sometimes the bouncers had to eject patrons. And just like any drunk who is tossed out of a bar, some of my thoughts were indignant! They did not believe the rules applied to them. Quite often, a thought would come back after it was asked nicely, or not so nicely, to leave.

I was forced to come up with a new and effective way to deal with these pesky little buggers. I found help in another most unusual idea. Paradoxically, giving troublesome patrons (persistent negative thoughts) permission to return was just the ticket. If a negative thought persisted in returning, I developed a three-strike rule: three strikes and you get permission. I would give that troublesome patron permission to return—tomorrow. I would tell the thought—through the bouncer, of course— that it could come back tomorrow; I was simply too busy to deal with it today. This worked almost every time. I discovered, quite to my delight, that my mind became less cluttered and more manageable. Slowly, but surely, I began to clean up the neighborhood.

Before I started this new thinking process, my mind was polluted with negativity and I did not want to spend any time in my head. It was definitely a bad neighborhood. I didn't care to go there, either alone or with friends. I discovered that if I wanted to be "happy, joyous, and free," ridding my thought process of unnecessary negativity was essential. Living in negativity was like trying to swim with concrete swim fins: It only dragged me down. While life isn't easy, and some negative things are bound to happen, I have discovered that much of what was wandering around in my head was not only unnecessary, it was useless dead weight. I needed to lighten the load.

Since I accept that some negative thoughts will always occur, when a thought reported to a bouncer, I would check to see if I classified it as either positive or negative. The positive thoughts were like the pretty girls who get to go to the head of the line (and who sometimes get into the club for free!), or handsome, prosperous-looking guys. Once inside, they were given free rein. However, the negative stuff was more like a scruffy, unwashed guy or girl trying to crash through the velvet rope. Those would-be patrons had only the slimmest chance of entering. The bouncers would make sure they were thoroughly checked before tossing them out.

This was time-consuming at first, but after a while it did not take me long to deal with any single thought. Like most humans, I'm capable of thinking very quickly; my problem was focus. My new goal was to focus on things that were necessary. In the beginning, positive thoughts were what I deemed necessary—it was that simple. But negative thoughts were given a chance to prove themselves worthy. I would ask them point-blank if they were necessary. The standard question was "Are you positive or negative?" followed by "Do I need to deal with you right this minute?" If I answered with a resounding "yes," then I would deal with the thought immediately. If my answer was "no" to the second question, or a sense of urgency could not be proven, I would have a bouncer escort the "patron" from the building.

Another quote from St. Francis of Assisi says, "Start by doing what's necessary, then do what's possible, and suddenly you are doing the impossible." By doing what was necessary—closely watching my thoughts—I learned it was possible to do so. By continuing to perform the activities I learned were possible, I did indeed do something I thought was impossible. I did become happy, joyous, and free. You are welcome to try the same thing for yourself. You too, can do the impossible. If not now, maybe later, but you can do anything you put your mind to, just as I did. For now, let's talk more about the process.

Being happy, joyous, and free is the result of a thought process. (Heavy emphasis is on process.) When I first began my journey toward happier thinking, I was exhausted by the end of the day. The bouncers were also pretty well exhausted by the end of the day, and I knew they could use some help. That's where upper management came in. Anything the bouncers couldn't handle got kicked upstairs to upper management. The job of upper management is to contain any thoughts that are so persistent as to be nearly unstoppable. When a thought returned after several attempts to reject or dismiss it, it got another chance to return the next day, and if it kept coming back, it would be referred to upper management. Upper management would then inform these pesky buggers that they could go form a committee somewhere out of the way—somewhere far removed from my conscious thinking process—to see if they could come up with a good enough reason to merit an audience with the club owner. This trick almost always worked. Upper management would escort the thought (patron) away with a firm grip, and, even though I knew it would be back, it wouldn't bother me anymore, for a while, at least. Still, this was strenuous work. My brain was exhausted. It felt as though it had been repeatedly poked with miniature, imaginary cattle prods. I was tired, but it was a good tired, and there was an upside. I slept very well. In fact, I slept better than I had in a long time. When I awoke most mornings, I felt refreshed and ready to take on the new day. I felt better than I had in years. Feeling better gave me the energy and the fortitude to carry on with the thought-monitoring process, even though it seemed it would wear me out. I hoped that in the long run I would create a new habit and learn to watch my thoughts without such exhaustive effort.

Hope paid off. Eventually I did form the habit of watching what I thought. Forming this habit did not take as long as I expected. After a week, I did not feel as tired at the end of the day. At first I took this to mean I was being lax in my practice of controlling access to my mind, so I reran the day's events to see if I had missed something. Of course, I couldn't rerun every thought, but I found this to be a good exercise. It was also a reinforcement of the fact that I had had a good day, for the most part. My thinking was clearing up gradually, and my actions were more in line with my desires. Instead of running through my day on autopilot, I had actually taken time to put thought into the things I had done. Every day I felt a little happier. The negativity was ever-so-slowly losing its grip.

After I spent a week doing my absolute best to rid my mind of unnecessary negativity, I felt happier. As a bonus, I found that without deliberately trying to find good things to think about, the action of removing negativity was creating a vacuum that soon filled with good and happy thoughts. In fact, what had once been a rather seedy nightclub was beginning to look more like an ice cream parlor, filled with wholesome, delicious treats instead of troublesome patrons looking to cause problems!

Looking back, this makes perfect sense. Without the negative thoughts, there was less to worry about; without the worry, my anxiety level plummeted rapidly. Things were looking good, so I decided to continue the process for a month.

At the end of the month, I felt so good I decided to add a wrinkle—inspired, but not directly suggested by my first sponsor: I made the decision to act as if everybody loved me. Some months earlier my sponsor had said, for seemingly no real reason I can recall, "Everybody loves me." When I finished laughing and noticed he wasn't laughing with me, I asked him how he could say such a thing. "I base this on the fact that no one has told me they don't love me," he said. While I hated to admit it, I had to agree with his logic. No one has ever told me they don't love me, either. While it would be impossible for everyone to tell me they do love me, I figured it would be an assumption worth making. I added his "enlightened understanding" of love and life to my new mind-watching program. If I treat everyone as though they love me, then I treat them better. If I treat people well, they treat me better. These days I treat everyone I love very well, so you can see the logic works. When people treat me better, it reinforces the entire process. Sure, some people didn't react positively to my new activities, but for the most part things went as I had hoped.

I did not do crazy things. After all, I was watching my thoughts. I did simple things at first. I said hello to strangers on the street. If you live in a very crowded city, it may be impossible to say hello to everyone. Even in a smaller city like the one I live in, it can begin to feel repetitive after a while, but it is not repetitive to the other person. It is the first time I have said hello to them all day (or maybe ever). I reminded myself of this fact and pressed forward, because people usually responded in kind, and many either smiled or added something extra such as a wink or a wave. A few people would actually begin a conversation, and, if we both had time, we would have a brief discussion. What a marvelous experience—the humanity of humankind.

So here I am, minding my own thought process, treating people as if they love me, and another month has gone by. I am happier, much more joyous, and freer than I have ever been. I decide another month of amazing growth is in order. What do I have to lose? As I am making the decision to go for month three, a thought hits me like a ton of bricks. I ask myself, "Who am I?" This question is followed with "Is this really me, and do I act like this?" A wave of negativity washed over me. I could never do this for the rest of my life. I could not possibly act as if everybody loved me forever. I cannot watch what I'm thinking forever, either. So why was I doing this? Well, the results spoke for themselves. I was reaching new heights, setting new goals, and living up to them. Life was truly becoming better. It wasn't great, but it was certainly better. Life was much better than it had been before, and, if I am completely honest, I was really enjoying myself. So I sent the negative thoughts to the bouncers to have them expelled. I still was not sure I could do it for the rest of my life but I knew that I could do it for another day—even another month—one day at a time. With the question of whether I was being true to who I was firmly implanted in my mind, I pressed on.

Another month passed, then another, and another. It has been a few years now. Many months have passed, a storehouse of twenty-four-hour periods. Each day was a new opportunity to do more and to do it better. I was getting to know myself one day at a time. In the process I discovered the reason I felt as though I wasn't being me in the beginning was that "I didn't know who I really was." How could I know me? I had never tried to in the past.

It took time to get used to the fact that I can know me—I should know me; I spend enough time with myself. Yes, it took time to get used to the new me. I am still getting used to me. I am a new person every day. It has been worth the time and effort without a doubt. Now that I know a bit more about myself, I can work on being true to myself. I can stand up for what I believe in, speak my mind—and know that I really know what I think—act the way I want, regardless of what other people may think or say about me.

I can be true to myself instead of trying to please others. I have found that, if I am true to myself, the reason I can do what I want to do—anything I want to do—is because I want to do good things. I want to do what is right, and when I think about what I am doing, I take others' feelings into account. It is the best I can do, I believe, to please others by considering their feelings before taking action. It is all part of being true to myself. If I am true to myself, I can be true to others.

I have discovered that I know the difference between right and wrong and that I have a strong desire to do right. I have come to believe the human tendency is to do right, and for all the years I was doing other than what is right, I was going against my true nature. In the process, I was feeding my disease with the "fuel of misbehavior." Having spent some time watching my thoughts, I have learned that I am not a bad person: I was either confused or I just did not bother to think about what I was doing. Maybe I didn't care enough to change. Today I do care. I want to be good and to do what is right. Along the way, I discovered this most basic of truths. I also found that I can not only watch my thoughts, I can change them, almost at will, and whenever I so desire. This realization took time and practice. It is yet another process. However, I believe it is a process well worth the effort.

I have learned it can be beneficial to change my thoughts on occasion, to change my mind, so to speak. When I do not like what I am thinking, I can change it if I want to. Sometimes this is more difficult than at other times, but it is always possible, and I have come up with a couple of "tricks" that work wonders for me.

The first trick is what I like to call "changing the station." The best example I know for explaining this one is when a song is trapped in my head. When it happens, I change the station! This is an easy process, and, while I had my doubts at first, I have found it to be effective in ridding myself of not just a song, but of nearly any undesirable thought I may find running laps in my brain while trying to wear me down. When I discover a song has taken up residence and will not stop its incessant clamor and its relentless attack upon my serenity, I quickly change the station. The first time I tried this, I lost the battle on several fronts before I finally succeeded in jettisoning the undesired tune. I figured I might be replacing the old song with another that would drive me just as crazy, but I found that what I chose as an alternate did not really want to be there.

Instead of complaining, I think of a song I do like. I begin to "sing" this new song in my head—I save the outside world the torture of my singing voice—and the song I like replaces the one I don't like. This has worked time and time again for me because I cannot keep two songs going at once. The new song goes away because it doesn't bother me. Because it no longer bothers me, I lose my focus on it. I cannot think of another way to explain the reason for its departure. I like the song and would not mind if it stayed around awhile, but it always goes away when its job is complete.

"Changing the station" led me to another idea, closely related to my replacement-song method. Occasionally, I find myself in an undesirable mood. This happened frequently in early recovery—not so much these days. I used to find that a bad mood could last for days. I could become depressed or mad, or experience any one of a number of negative emotions. I would wallow in a foul mood, and for extended periods. Like the song I disliked, the mood would stay until it decided to leave. No more! I can rid myself of a bad or sad mood very quickly if I want to.

I devised a simple plan for addressing the bad moods that appeared and tried to make themselves at home in my mind. And I have used this plan successfully on many occasions. The trick is to enjoy the mood. The first question that arose when I came up with this idea was: "How do I enjoy being depressed?" The answer is, I don't *really* so much enjoy it as I give myself permission to be depressed. I decide to be depressed as long as I want to. However, I take the time to feel depressed. First, I know it will pass eventually. If I give myself permission to feel depressed instead of trying to be something else, the depression seems to last a much shorter time. The act of "granting myself permission" has an immediate effect on the feeling. Just as the undesirable song that becomes lodged in my head stays because I don't want it there, I replace it with a song I prefer and which I give permission to take its place. This seems to alleviate the condition—giving a mood permission to stay, and really feeling that mood, this seems to facilitate the mood or feeling's expedited departure.

The effect seems to be threefold. First, I approach it by feeling—I mean really feeling—the mood. I was so used to running from feelings and moods that the habit became chronic, but I came to understand that feelings won't kill me, so why should I not want to feel them? The act of feeling leads directly to step two, which is "giving permission." I decide to be depressed, or whatever my current mood happens to be. Through this, I come to realize that since I am giving permission to this feeling, I can decide to feel otherwise whenever I choose, but I do not want to rush the process. I am not trying to avoid the feeling. I am simply choosing to work my way through it instead of allowing it to decide what I will do. Finally, I reach acceptance: I simply accept that this is part of being human. I do not wish things were different. I do not wish that I were happy. I just know I will be happy soon, when I am finished feeling whatever it is I am feeling at this moment. It can take a while to get used to this process. It may seem a little weird at first, but this works for me, and it can work for you.

I learned these tricks by monitoring my thought process. It took time for me to learn how I think. You can do it also. You can make changes and improve upon these methods. In fact, if you are willing to give these suggestions a try, I am almost certain that you will discover secrets about yourself and the way you think that will change your life for the better. The key to uncovering the truth is to learn how you think. Once I knew the way I thought, I could change my thought process and adapt it as I saw fit. This takes time, but I'm not in a hurry. Time marches on, whether I am practicing new habits or repeating old behaviors resulting in less than optimal results. I wanted new results, so I looked for new activities. When I found something that worked, I put it into practice.

Practice is the key. Practice makes progress, but does not make perfect. There will be mistakes and failures along the way, but failure is not the end—it is just the beginning. A wise man once said, "Failure is simply the opportunity to begin again, this time more intelligently." I try something new; if it works, great; if it doesn't work, I learn from it. Then I try again, or I try something else new. That's life. Along the way, I ask for help and advice because I know how beneficial it can be to ask for help with things with which I am unfamiliar. However, it is still up to me to practice the things that work while learning from the things that do not work. In the meantime, I do my best to take things as they come, which leads to the next thinking opportunity.

I remember telling my first sponsor, on one occasion in particular, about a situation I thought was going to happen. I described the situation at the current time and gave him all the facts as I saw them. The situation, as I saw it, was undesirable, and, to be honest, I wished things were different. I was feuding with the woman in my life, and it looked like there was a big fight coming down the pike. After I gave my sponsor the facts of my situation, I said, "If she does this, I'm going to do that. If she does so and so, I'm going to do such and such." My sponsor was visibly amused.

"Don't make up your mind about something that hasn't happened yet," he said, and I fell silent. I had no idea what this could possibly mean. I was planning my course of action. I was preparing for the future. I was wasting time, energy, and effort. I just did not know it yet. The more I thought about what he had said, the more I realized how right he was. All I was really doing was worrying. I was making predictions and reacting to them. What a waste of life.

Predictions are generally erroneous, and most often lead to nothing more than headaches, especially when my predictions involve what other people will think or how they will act. I have found that I am often wrong about these things regardless of how well I know the person. As I pondered this thought, I discovered that even when my intentions were to be kind and good, things often did not go the way I figured. I cannot count the number of times I planned to take my ex-wife out for dinner while visualizing just how happy that would make her. I thought she would relish the opportunity to be catered to for the evening, but I discovered that her day had been a total drain on her, and all she wanted to do was stay home and relax. Since this was usually a blow to me, I usually acted in ways that were less than helpful. After all, *I* had made up my mind. We were going out to dinner and it was a good thing. Little did I know. While this is an example of good intentions gone awry, I did enjoy the elaborate planning involved in my scenario. I had a good time imagining what the future might hold. The letdown did not come until later. The same cannot be said for imagining potential conflict.

Imagining a future conflict is nothing more than counterproductive and a total waste of time. I have looked for, and not been able to find, a situation where living, thinking about, contemplating, preparing for, or doing anything with regard to future conflict is productive or normal in everyday life. What this exercise in futility usually does is ruin my present moment with potential future conflict—conflict that most likely will never come to pass. I have heard it said, "I have lived a life of many troubles, most of which have never happened." The message of that saying is clear. I base most of my worries on a concern for what has not yet happened, and the vast majority of my concerns will never come to pass.

As an example, I was planning for a battle, a conflict, so to speak, and I played out the scenario in my mind. I did not like the way it played out, so I tried another scenario when the previous one proved unsatisfactory. I tried a third scenario, and still had no luck. I played and replayed possible scenarios for hours. In the end, I had entertained at least a dozen different possibilities. I found that most, if not all, of them were to be less than appealing. There were a couple of potential outcomes that could have been fun, if my idea of fun was causing the other person great pain. However, I was doing my best to be a better person, as I am trying to do today, so I was less than enthusiastic about the potential conflict. Finally, the time came. I was watching to see which of my possible scenarios would come to pass. What I didn't realize at the time (but which I do know today) is that no matter how many scenarios I run through, only one will actually happen. Therefore, if I visited a dozen, I wasted time on eleven. In this particular instance, there was no battle. All my time was wasted on needless worry. The other person had been wrong—something I had self-righteously believed all along—and came to apologize. I had planned, schemed, and wasted my entire day. On top of that, I felt like an idiot for not seeing what was to transpire. At this point, I was left with a lose/lose situation.

The good news is that I forgave the person who had wronged me, and I learned a lesson. My sponsor was right. There was no need to make up my mind based upon events that had not yet happened. If I had waited for the actual event to take place and enjoyed the time leading up to the confrontation by occupying my mind with pleasant thoughts, when the time came for the potential conflict, I would have been in a much better state of mind. I would have been able to enjoy the fact that the other person was willing to admit their mistake. I would have been able to forgive them more freely because I would not have felt bad about being wrong about them and their ability to apologize, and I would not have wasted my day mired in worry and fear.

Today, instead of seeking conflict, I search for a workable solution. I have found that looking for the right solution is good. If I want to be happy—truly happy—I have no mind-space available for seeking revenge, reliving the wrongs of the past—self-inflicted or otherwise—or trying to figure out what I will do if someone else does something I do not like. "If" seldom ever comes to pass.

Instead of looking for what is wrong, I must look for what is right. While every cloud has a silver lining, this is no reason to walk around with my head in the clouds. Instead, it is a call for solutions. The Bible says, "Seek and ye shall find." My question today is: "What do I want to find?"

Learning how I think is a twenty-four-hour-a-day practice—fewer than that if I count time off for sleep, but I always remember to count my dreams. I'm not into interpreting dreams. I simply have a new attitude about them. So I count my "dream time" as part of the practice, and I call it practice instead of work. I count dreams because they used to freak me out sometimes.

When I had drinking dreams during my early recovery, I would sometimes wake up in a near panic wondering if I had actually gotten drunk. Over time I have changed my attitude about dreams, and, therefore, how I react to those I have. These days when I have a drinking dream I know it is a dream because I know I do not drink. Quite often, I am aware that I am having a dream while I am having the dream. By practicing the mental monitoring process, I have trained myself to watch for thoughts of drinking. When awake, if I have a thought that is similar to "Wouldn't a beer taste good right now?" I respond to it with a firm "I do not drink alcohol. Begone, negative thought." In this way, I reinforce in my mind the fact that I no longer participate in the consumption of alcoholic beverages. This seems to have carried over to my dream state, because when I have a drinking dream nowadays I watch it like a movie—

to see what will happen next—as opposed to letting it put me into a panic. I know I do not drink. Therefore, if I am drinking, then this must be a dream. There is more to it than simple awareness. In order to overcome the fear of drinking dreams, which I have actually come to enjoy to some extent, I had to learn to relax my mind while I was awake.

I used to panic when faced with a decision. Almost any decision I had to make could strike fear in my heart. This reaction occurred because I thought I had to give an answer or make a decision on the spot. I have changed this bad habit. Today I refuse to make snap decisions. My first sponsor told me he had a policy on making snap decisions. If a person asked him a question, he would tell him or her, "If you have to know right now, the answer is no; however, if you are willing to wait and give me a chance to think it over, that might change." He said he used this answer whenever he felt pressured to make a choice. He also told me his policy was to avoid decisions that could prove to be life-changing without sleeping on them for at least one night. He shared a personal experience with me, and I think it is a good example of how to do the right thing by not making a "snap" decision.

An asphalt company was repaving the road in front of his house. At the same time, they were going door-to-door giving a "great price" on repaving driveways. The price, they said, was so good because they were already there and could do it the same day, but they had to know his answer "right now." He told them if they had to know right now the answer was no, but if they could wait until the next day for the answer, it might change. They left without an arrangement to repave his driveway, but many of my sponsor's neighbors took the deal and were disappointed.

The job was poorly done, probably because the workers were in a hurry to complete the work. In no time, the newly repaved driveways were cracking. It didn't matter whether or not my sponsor's neighbors were able to get their money back, or to have the work repaired or replaced; my sponsor did not have to experience the worry and headache of dealing with the issue. The lesson, he taught me, was to "give the mind time to think."

Snap decisions often lead to trouble, or at least to making bad choices we wish we had the opportunity to do over. In life we seldom get a "do-over." Put another way, "act in haste, repent at leisure."* I have put this practice to work in my life and found it bears fruit. In fact, I rarely make a decision without sleeping on it if I think it could have long-term effects. What I will have for dinner is not something to sleep on. But whether or not I should buy a new car is! After giving myself time to ponder this new outlook on life and think about making choices, I decided that anything costing over a certain dollar amount or anything that would require more than a certain amount of time would require sleep. In fact, the more it cost, or the more of my time it would require, the longer I would take to make the decision, and the longer I would sleep on the idea. I have taken days, even weeks, to make up my mind about what to do about, or how to approach, situations since I have adopted this new practice, and it has paid wonderful dividends. I have modified my original quotas as time has passed, but the basics remain the same. I no longer rush my brain in a futile attempt to force results. To do so is foolish.

*The actual proverb is "marry in haste," but the principle is the same.

I have learned to follow my wandering mind to watch what it does. I do not have to be in the lead when it comes to making choices. I feel no need to "tell my mind what to think." I let my mind do its job and then I make my choice. This works well for me; just how well it works has come to light in many fascinating ways.

I took a writing class not too long ago, during which the instructor introduced the idea that writing is a process. It's a process with several individual steps—in the "prewriting" phase the mind needs time to come up with an idea about which to write; then, in the draft phase, more time is required to organize the idea into a comprehensive format. Writing in these phases should spark the mind into action. However, the final product will improve with age. As I allow my brain to process information on the original topic, things begin to come into focus. Following the process through the editing and publication, or sharing, phases, I find I soon have a fully formed product. Like many other things, ideas get old and either spoil or die; when they do, they must be processed properly. According to this process, it is important to practice the fine art of following the mind around to see how it is working and to keep an eye on ideas to see "when they are done." With practice and patience, this process becomes second nature.

While learning to follow my mind as it journeys to new and exciting places, I realized I was learning how my mind works. The human brain is complex, and everyone's brain works a little differently. Your brain will tell you when a decision has been reached. One guideline I use to determine when I've reached a decision is that if I do not know what to do, I don't do anything. If there is any doubt, I wait. As I wait, I watch. I watch my thinking and I watch the situation. Sometimes the situation will change to the extent that no action on my part is even required. However, if action on my behalf is required, it will become clear to me what action I should take. When I am patient with an opportunity, an issue, or a problem, I find the answer comes more easily if I allow my brain to process the information in the above-mentioned way.

I seek solutions from within. I allow them to come forward. I cannot count the number of times I have run around the house looking for something I have misplaced—my keys or wallet—with no positive results, only to give up the search and sit in my chair disgruntled, wondering what I could possibly have done with the item. I may have spent several minutes to an hour in search of the missing article; then, having given up, I remember where it is. How can this be? Simple: I relaxed my brain. I quit trying to force an answer, and, in removing the force, I allowed the brain to work at its own speed and to think for me.

The answers may amaze you if you are willing to let the mind do its job. While it may seem counterproductive to sit on my butt when I should be looking for something, I can often save time by simply taking a moment to relax. It is also important to remember that the more difficult the issue, the longer it can take the brain to process the information. Because of this, I have found it advantageous to put things out of my mind—to the best of my ability—while it is working on them. What I am really doing in these situations is getting out of my own way. When I say I put them out of my mind, what I mean is that I stop forcing my mind to contemplate the particular item at hand. I let the mind do what it has to do. I have faith in it to report back when it has arrived at a solution. I am able to relieve the stress I have created and allow the mind to do its job without my interference.

I view my mind like any other working situation. If my boss watches me too closely—hovering over me—then my ability to perform suffers. At worst, I will get nothing done at all while he is hounding me. When he walks away, I get busy. When the pressure eases, I can work more efficiently. My brain is the same way. It just wants me to go away so it can work. Today, I do my best to allow this to happen. I have enough faith in my mind to know the answer will come to me when it is ready. This faith didn't come overnight. It took practice letting my mind do its job and report back, and it took trust that it would happen. However, it does work. It works better the more I trust it, and I trust it more as I use it. This is one of those upward spirals—positive results begetting positive actions, and positive actions begetting positive results. It's the opposite of what I practiced for many years. The results can come slowly at first, but they will come if I am willing to do my part. It works best if I remain calm. I find it easiest to remain calm if I can stop creating my own emergencies.

The first step to becoming a more peaceful person is to realize that, in most cases, I am creating my own emergencies. Often I am so enmeshed in the results that I do not plan properly. Other times I convince myself that I am supposed to be living in the present, to the point where I forget I must be willing to plan a course of action before I can take appropriate steps to accomplish a task. At other times, I look at a project and become overwhelmed by the vastness of its complexity, forgetting that it can be broken down into manageable parts. In any of these scenarios, I am creating an emergency of some sort. An emergency is an urgent need for action, a situation that I deem to require urgent action. While the situations I think of as emergencies are of a serious nature, like cutting my finger or a more serious form of physical harm, some emergencies are of a more subtle, yet more paralyzing nature. If I see something that I must deal with so quickly that I forget to make a plan for dealing with it properly, I can make things worse by taking quick, yet incorrect, action. Failing to plan is always the same as planning to fail. Whether I am caught up in the outcome or trying hard to remain in the present, I sometimes forget to make a plan, and by doing so set myself up for failure. If, on the other hand, I view a situation as insurmountable, I may simply give up before I even try. Even though the task is one that must be done, I will sit and do nothing while things get worse. Planning is an essential part of action. Action is required for results. Both planning and action are necessary to achieve positive outcomes.

Having a proper plan makes some projects possible, and it makes other tasks easier. However, a plan is required for almost any assignment, no matter who assigned it. Sometimes projects come with a plan, like a model airplane or a work-related assignment. Other times, I must create the plan myself. In fact, if the project is one of my own, I am required to devise a plan of some sort. The key is to plan how I am to go about accomplishing the task, not what will happen later. The results are usually not up to me. I can have as many expectations as I want, but they may not come to fruition. I have found that if I want to carry around large quantities of expectations, I should also have an equal or greater amount of acceptance so I can deal with the potential fallout. The key to success is to plan to the best of my ability, execute the plan as best I can, then see what happens in order to begin the next plan, instead of worrying about what may or may not happen.

Worrying is a way of creating false emergencies and troubles. Through worry I can end the world as I know it, if I carry the worry far enough. I am sure you have heard, "If I pray, why worry, and if I worry, why pray?" I like to think of every thought as a prayer. That way, when I am worrying, I am praying and I am praying negatively. I have found the best way to stop worry is to plan, act, and then see what happens. Then make another plan, a new one to fit the new situation.

Prayer always helps, but worry is not good prayer. Instead of living in my head, wondering and worrying about what will happen, I make a plan and follow it through—making adjustments as necessary—to see what happens. The actual results are not what I expected, so why should I be concerned with outcomes? If I trust God to make all things work for good, then even if I make a horrid mistake, He will help straighten things out. He will provide me with a better plan—quite often through the results of the last plan. "Stop worrying" is much easier said than done. This doesn't mean I try to stop worrying altogether. (I could end up worrying about how much I worry if I did that!) What I like to do is to recognize what my worry looks like, and take action to alleviate it. Making a plan is one way to do this. Another way is through categorization.

I can choose to categorize thoughts as true or false. I discard emergencies I categorize as false; however, in order to do this I must first learn to categorize them. The simplest way to do this is to ask myself, "Is this a real emergency?" While this may sound so simple as to render itself ineffective, the results can be quite amazing. I know right from wrong and good from bad. I also know true from false. I can tell the difference between a true emergency and a false one in most cases. The problem arises when I do not allow myself time to perform the act of categorization. Today, whenever I find I am in a quandary, I ask myself,

"Is this truly an emergency, or am I getting worked up over something imagined?" If I am honest with myself, I usually know the answer. If I cannot answer for myself, I ask for help in making a determination. Asking for help is important in these cases, because if I really do not know, I can make something into more than it deserves to be, which is a waste of time.

Once I discard false emergencies, I free up time to deal with the real ones. Sometimes I have to spend time to save time—like looking for my keys. Spending time trying to figure out which are real emergencies and which are not is time well spent. Freeing my mind from the encumbrance of false emergencies allows me to think more clearly and helps me to see life more as it is, instead of wallowing in the mystifying falsehood of make-believe "realities." If I am to deal with life on life's terms, I need to know what those terms really are. I cannot afford to become bogged down with imaginings about what reality might be. "What could happen," "If only," "I wish," and the like must be dealt with properly in order for me to move forward.

Real emergencies occur much more rarely than I am used to thinking they do, because I was so used to living in the emergencies I made up. Once I learned to identify and discard the false emergencies I created, I discovered that "true emergencies" are far rarer than I had ever expected. I can become quite adept at distinguishing between reality and falsity; in the process I can calm my life down to a level that allows me to deal with it in positive way, instead of feeling as though I am always running around trying to put out fires.

I must strive for serenity, not chaos, for in serenity come answers, solutions, plans, and positive results. In serenity, even failure can be a good thing, because it is a beginning, not an end. When I am serene, I take life more in stride and my thinking is more on an even keel, more processed, less anguished, more polished, and more complete. When I maintain serenity, I can see that my thinking is a productive process. I can learn the way it works, and I can change how I think, what I think about, and even "what I think" about how and what I think. By learning about my thinking process I can see how it affects the way I feel, and I can learn to make changes when appropriate. There are so many advantages to watching how I think that probably the greatest is finding a little serenity, learning to be less affected—even unaffected—by happenings around me. I am unique in my thinking. I can use it for good rather than beat myself up for not thinking like everyone else. I can be myself and allow, even encourage, others to be themselves. I can lose my fear of feeling unique. That's right—I once feared being unique.

Being unique is a good thing when properly understood. Human beings are simultaneously alike and unique. We each have unique fingerprints, perceptions, and outlooks on life. While we share many commonalities, we are also quite different. One of the biggest differences may be the way we think. I often ask people I trust to check my thinking by running ideas past them for their input. I do this because I value their ideas, the way they think. I do not value their thinking because it is the same as mine, but because it is different. If they always give me the same ideas I already have, why do I need to ask for their help? It is through our uniqueness that we can offer new views on life, and receive new views as well. I used to think my uniqueness made me weird, odd, or wrong. Today, I think it makes me normal. I am unique, just like everybody else.

In order to use my uniqueness properly, I had to stop the negative thinking. I had to dispel the notion that because my thinking is different it must be wrong. My thinking is no more wrong than is anyone else's. Sure, I can stand to improve my thinking—who could not use a little improvement?

Today I am doing the best I can to eliminate negative thinking from my life. In doing so, I am helping to clean up the neighborhood in which I live—the neighborhood of my mind. It is a neighborhood where I will reside for the rest of my life. I have found that the more effort I put into this project, the better the results and the more I come to like my new neighborhood. I can go there alone and without fear. In fact, I often go there just to visit, to see what will happen next, to watch the action—to learn who I am and who I am becoming. The best part, though, is that nowadays I don't just go into my mind to visit, I go there to live.

TODAY I CHOOSE TO BE

HAPPY, JOYOUS, AND FREE,

AND HAVE NO DESIRE TO

DRINK. TO DESIRE IS TO WISH

OR LONG FOR. IT IS A WASTE

OF TIME AND ENERGY THAT

LEADS TO NOTHING BUT PAIN

AND SUFFERING FOR SOMEONE

WITH MY CONDITION.

INSTEAD, I WANT A HAPPY

LIFE, ONE I CAN HAVE

IF I BELIEVE I CAN.

5

BELIEFS

The differences between "I think" and "I believe" are subtle, yet important. While we often use the two interchangeably in everyday conversation, it is important for me to pay attention to how I use "I believe" in any form of communication. Many things that I believe today I learned while growing up. Others I have picked up in school, from scientific studies or reports, from books I have read, or even from my own ideas about how life is or should be. While the dictionary uses "to believe or suppose" as one definition for "think," as in "It is later than you might think," and the two words can be used synonymously, I will use the following definition for belief: "mental acceptance of and conviction in the truth, actuality, or validity of something." Beliefs are something we accept as correct or true in life. I believe the way we use the word believe (or belief) is important to how we approach everyday life. If I treat what I believe casually, my beliefs will usually collapse under very little evidence to the contrary, or wander and stray nearly at random. Beliefs should not do this. What I believe is a large part of who I am and how I act, and I should take it very seriously. For a day, a week, or a month, take a good look at how you use "I believe" in your everyday conversation. Knowing how you use the term may give you insight into how strong your belief system really is, and whether you might benefit by taking a serious look at how you think about your beliefs.

I came across my difficulty with the terms "I think" and "I believe" as I began to monitor my thinking process. I discovered that I used "think" and "believe" interchangeably—my actual beliefs were very weak in most cases—and that I held very few strong convictions about anything. Looking back over my life, it is not hard to see why this happened. Things change all the time, and it seems that just when I start believing something, someone comes along with evidence to the contrary. When my disease was active, I would take this or that person, scientific study, or whatever at their word. I would avoid doing any homework on the subject, I'd change my beliefs, and I would do so quite often without giving it any genuine thought. (The only real belief I held was that I would continue getting loaded.) Everything else was up in the air, and why not? This month the news said eggs were bad for me; the next month they were good. One day, recycling is something everyone needs to do; the next thing I know, it is so difficult to recycle that no one is doing it. The whims of man and science had me completely baffled. I really did not know what to believe, except that I would have another drink. In this way, I was able to simplify my life and avoid needless worry.

Since I stopped using, many things have changed, especially when it comes to my beliefs. I have taken ownership of what I believe. Much of what I believe today flies in the face of what is "popular" to believe, now that I am thinking for myself, doing some research, checking things out, and making my own decisions. I've come to believe that "popular" belief, popular music, popular clothes, and popular people do not generally last very long. Since I am tired of changing my beliefs every time someone else says I should, today my beliefs are hard-won. I do not just believe something I am told by others is true. If you want a great example of falsehoods taken as fact, consider your email. How much of it do you believe to be true and how much can stand up to investigation? I always check out email I receive to determine whether it is true before I will send it on to my list of friends. I know much of what I receive in my email box is a fabrication. With the possible exception of a few trusted friends, I remain skeptical until I check it out myself. This may sound extreme, but when it comes to what I believe, it is necessary to check the details first, because the things I believe drive my behavior whether they are true or not.

I used for years beyond when I could have sought help, because I believed I could stop any time I wanted. I continued to use because I believed it was what I was supposed to do. Birds fly, fish swim, addicts use, right? Finally, I also believed quitting would be the end of my world. My beliefs drove my behavior, even though these beliefs were based on fiction. Fortunately, when it came to my drinking and drugging, my belief that quitting would be the end of my world would prove wrong. I put up a good, hard fight before anyone would prove me wrong on this. I held out as long as I could—even in the face of proper evidence—because I believed that I would rather be loaded than boring, or whatever it was that had me scared to death about being clean and sober. My beliefs were very strong, and they drove my behavior.

Today, I treat my beliefs as though they have the same power as my drinking once did because all evidence points to this being the truth. Before I will allow myself to form a new belief or change one that I currently hold, I do some investigation. I check the facts to see if it might be worthwhile to take on a new set of beliefs. There are many ways to go about investigating facts. Depending on the situation, I employ the tactics I deem necessary. The most important thing I do is the homework. Then I do some thinking. If necessary, I do more research and more thinking. The point is, I make up my own mind about what I believe based on facts as they present themselves, and upon my goals.

My goals often drive my beliefs. Therefore, I must take care in identifying them. If my goals are simply to get clean and sober and stay clean and sober, then I may simply not pick up—anything. However, if my goals are to become a better, more happy, and caring person, I will need a larger set of beliefs. One goal encompasses becoming happy and caring. In order to develop these new beliefs, I will most likely need help, but I must be cautious in how I seek help, for there are advantages to using caution.

Seeking advice and counsel is good. However, blindly following others' advice can create dependence. If I simply do what other people tell me to do and believe what other people tell me is true, I will not learn to think for myself. I will not grow in my ability to make my own decisions and I will not learn to determine what I believe. Instead, I will believe what others believe, and there is no advantage in doing such a thing. This kind of "blind faith" can lead me into all kinds of trouble. My belief system will become dependent upon what other people believe, and when they change what they believe, I will simply follow along. I will not be living my own life, and odds are I will be following "popular belief" into a cycle of changing convictions. I also will not learn the art of thinking for myself, and if I do not practice thinking, I will never become a good thinker. I will not be able to monitor my thinking process, because I won't really have one. I will be thinking what other people tell me to think because I will believe what they tell me to believe. Oh, I will have my own thoughts, but they will revolve around what other people believe, not what I hold to be true. Seeking counsel should be done quite often, yet with great care. Upon receiving counsel, I must consider what I think about the advice, do some homework if necessary, spend some time making up my own mind, and then decide what I believe.

I must do this because I tend to follow my beliefs—consciously or not—with my actions. My beliefs drive my actions. I should never allow someone else to dictate my actions by indoctrinating me with their beliefs. I must learn to make my own decisions when it comes to what I believe. This takes persistence and practice—some might even call it work—but it is well worth the effort to become a whole person.

Some beliefs are so ingrained that I do not give them much thought. Generally, this is true because the belief is based on solid fact. For instance, I believe the sun will come up tomorrow. Because I do, I act accordingly. I go to bed, get a good night's sleep, and plan for my future. Consider, for a moment, what might happen and how I might act if I did not believe this—if somehow I became convinced the sun would not come up tomorrow. I might conclude that the world would end, because without heat from the sun the Earth, and everyone on it, would freeze. I might do any number of things I would not normally do if I were to hold the belief that the sun would not rise tomorrow. I might spend the night calling family and friends—or driving to their houses—or I might stay up all night watching for the telltale signs of a sunrise. However, I would most likely not go to bed, not plan for the future, and not get a good night's sleep. This example may sound a little far-fetched because the sun will most assuredly come up tomorrow; still, it does make a point. I can reach the point where I do not really give my belief a second thought.

When I quit drinking and drugging and began to take a careful look at how I think and what I believe, I discovered I had thoughts and beliefs to which I did not give a second glance, even though they were making life much more difficult. What I decided to do, which came from monitoring my thoughts, was to take a look at what I believe, because I realized my beliefs hold an abundance of sway over my life. What I discovered in looking into what I believe is that I held many false beliefs. I still acted in ways that were counter to the way I wanted to live my life as an upstanding member of society. At first I wondered how this could be, but after contemplation and some research I discovered a new truth regarding my becoming a person in recovery. It was an amazing, yet simple, discovery that changed my outlook: I cannot "just have one."

When our behavior gets better—when we quit using—a shift in our belief system must follow close behind, or we will fall back into our old behaviors in order to meet our old beliefs. As I studied this idea, I observed that many of my old beliefs about using and being in recovery had survived my trip into recovery. I found this out because I still on occasion thought I could "have just one beer." This is really the assertion of my old belief that "I can quit whenever I choose." This is an example of my thinking (I can have one beer) following my beliefs (old beliefs) that had become so ingrained in my life that the thought "magically appears" in my head. It comes out of nowhere. Isn't that what I hear from people in the program? Isn't that what I still believed? These crazy thoughts about having a cold beer came out of nowhere. I do not believe that anymore. They are, after all, in my mind, and if they are there, then I am sure there is a reason. I am just as sure that the reason they're there is because I still hold the belief that I can quit anytime I want.

With time, these beliefs change. I begin to understand that I cannot have "just one." However, for a long time I never addressed my old belief that I could quit anytime I wanted, so the thought of using seemed to return with regularity. With simple treatment, through watching my thoughts, I was able for the most part to dismiss this idea. Sometimes I had to call my sponsor or find another way to deal with the thought, but for the most part I could simply dismiss it and it would disperse. With practice, the frequency of using thoughts lessened and it became easier to disregard their intrusion into my life, but they still showed up too often for my liking. When I finally addressed the basic belief that I could stop anytime I wanted, I received relief beyond imagination.

Many people might say this is done by "playing the tape all the way through" in my mind, to visualize what happens when I pick up a drink, a pill, anything. I will not argue whether "playing the tape" works. I have seen it work too often to doubt. In "playing the tape," we are changing our belief about being able to stop drinking anytime we desire. When I recall the misery of my using and how it all started with one drink, I see that time and again I was unable to stop when I wanted. With repetition, I reinforce the truth about my disease and I change my belief about my condition. Finally, I begin to accept the fact I am an addict, that I cannot stop when I want, and in the process address the underlying belief that I can stop whenever I choose. I replace the old belief that I can quit with the belief that once I take a substance, choice goes out the window.

When I accept the fact that I cannot control my using, that I cannot stop when I want, I change my belief; when I change my belief about this fact, my life becomes easier. This acceptance takes time and practice. However, acceptance is the key to changing my beliefs; accepting the truth of my disease is crucial to my recovery. Once I accepted that I could not stop using once I started, it became easier to dismiss the thought of having "just one." As my acceptance grew, my beliefs in this area changed. Until this happened, I had difficulty with the idea that I had a using (or stopping) problem. However, once I came to accept the truth about my disease, and my belief system underwent a change, it became a normal part of my life to refuse not only a substance but also the thought of having "just one."

Do you hate people who say, "I don't need (or want) a drink/pill/joint/whatever"? Well, I have become one of those people. I have done so for two reasons that quickly come to mind. First, it is easier—in fact, possible—for me to live a happy life when I don't use. Second, I have found it to be detrimental to me to hate anything. For example, I can choose to object to, disapprove of, or take exception to the fact that other people can drink and that I cannot, but I do so at the peril of my own serenity. I have found it easiest to simply accept the fact that some people can consume alcohol and some people cannot, and I am one who cannot (without suffering severe consequences). Because I am one who cannot, I choose to not want to. I find it is healthier for me to not want to use than to wrestle with the facts. I have changed my attitude when it comes to drinking and all other manifestations of my disease, and with my new attitude, I have changed my beliefs regarding alcohol. This is true because I believe it to be true. I believe it to be true because I have fully accepted the truth regarding my disease.

For me the truth is that I used to need to drink; that changed when I quit drinking. After a period of withdrawal, I no longer needed to drink to stave off the discomfort of withdrawal. However, I still had a problem because I still wanted to drink. I wanted to be able to drink like a social drinker—that is, like other people. But today, I don't even want to. I will admit a large part of the reason I do not want to be able to drink like other people—like social drinkers—is because I now know I can't, but that does not change the fact that I have come to believe I no longer want to drink. I simply know the true nature of my condition, accept the facts as they are, and then deal with the truth in a way that is most beneficial to my health and my well-being. I no longer fight with the desire to drink. I do not want to fight anymore, so I don't. In order to accomplish this, I changed my beliefs. I believe I am alcoholic; alcoholics don't drink (drunks do), and I do not drink alcohol. I have no desire to drink alcohol. I have stopped wishing I could drink like other people, and that has changed my life. I enjoy drinking water, lemonade, 7-Up, and iced tea. I also enjoy having my brain to myself instead of wondering what it may be up to, which is exactly what I was doing during my drinking days. I no longer want the repercussions and consequences that drinking brought about. What I truly believe will dominate my life. What I focus my attention on will, for the most part, come to pass. I used to focus on drinking. I used to spend nearly twenty-four hours a day obsessed with alcohol. If I was not drinking, I was either drunk or thinking about getting drunk, sleeping off a drunk, or nursing a hangover. My life used to revolve around alcohol.

Today, my life revolves around recovery and helping others to recover. Doing the next right thing, taking other people's feelings into account before I act, doing the best job I can when I am working and enjoying myself in the process, enjoying the moment when I am playing, and enjoying the friends I am playing with are very important to me. Today I choose to be happy, joyous, and free, and have no desire to drink. To desire is to wish or long for. It is a waste of time and energy that leads to nothing but pain and suffering for someone with my condition. Instead, I want a happy life, one I can have if I believe I can.

My first sponsor used to say he was "happy, joyous, and free" every single time I asked him how he was doing, and since I called him every day for the entire time I knew him—that was a lot! (I didn't know then, or for some time, that these words first appeared in *Alcoholics Anonymous*, the basic text of the organization that bears that name.)

This used to drive me crazy, probably because, in early recovery, I wanted to be happy, joyous, and free; I just did not know how. Finally, I could take it no longer. I asked him how it was he could be happy, joyous, and free all the time, because I certainly wasn't. I was closer to miserable, and I did not enter recovery to be miserable. If I wanted to be miserable, I could go get loaded—that always brought me great misery. But I wanted to be happy, joyous, and free, and here I was, talking to a guy who not only claimed to be just what I was looking for, but he actually seemed to be happy, joyous, and free. Every time I saw him, he was smiling. It drove me nuts. I asked him how he could be happy, joyous, and free all the time, especially with all the aches and pains a person must have when he or she is ninety-plus years old. He said, "I claim it, then I live it."

I was thoroughly baffled by his statement. I went home to think about it, mostly because I knew he would tell me to go home and think about it if I asked him to explain. He always told me to go home and think about things before we would discuss them. I disliked the delayed gratification at the time. However, the practice at delaying gratification, as well as the practice at thinking, have been a real boon to my recovery. Today, I highly recommend both to anyone I sponsor, and I do my best to give them something to think about; then I let them think it over.

I went home and thought for what seemed like a month, but was probably only a week, before I broached the subject again. To be honest, I probably did not do much thinking on the subject. I was newly sober; however, I could not forget the topic since he brought it up every time I talked with him, and I really did have a desire to be happy, joyous, and free. I brought it up again. I told him I had thought about it and I still did not understand what he meant by "claim it and live it." He explained, "When I wake up in the morning, I claim it; as I go through my day, I live it." He then told me to go try it. More delayed gratification... gotta love it.

Even though what I really wanted was for him to give me happiness in a neat little gift-wrapped box, I decided I was willing to do some work to attain happiness because I saw the results in my sponsor. I saw him nearly every day for a year and a half and I knew, even during the first six months, that I would be willing to work hard for the results he had attained. We went to meetings together at least five days a week. I tried because I was willing to do the work, but I also wanted to be able to say I had tried: "I tried that; it didn't work." I tried for a week; a month; still nothing. I was the same old me, just poking along in life, staying sober and struggling to make progress. I brought up the subject again at the end of that month. (Have I mentioned that a month was the length of time he liked me to try new things?) "Do it for a month; if you don't like it, you can quit," was his standard reply to "How long should I do this?"

At the end of the month, I brought it up again by telling him that I had gained little or no ground. I had claimed it, but I could not quite get the hang of living it. Every morning when I woke up I would claim to be happy, joyous, and free, but soon enough I would slip back into grumpy. "Soon enough?" he asked with a chuckle. "How long are you happy before you slip back into grumpy?"

"It varies," I admitted, "Some days I may be happy for an hour, some days maybe half a day, but I have never made it a whole day. Something always comes along to ruin my mood." "There is your problem," he claimed with a grin. "It is *your* mood. How can something else ruin it?"

I had to admit he was right. It is my mood. From this discussion, I learned being happy is a choice. From changing my thinking, which happened more than a year later—ridding myself of negative thoughts to a large extent—I learned that much of what I think is the thing that bears on my happiness. However, it wasn't until I reached my beliefs that I really made happiness permanent.

Today I am happy because I believe I am happy. What I truly believe has begun to dominate my life. This happened because I tend to find evidence to support the belief. This is yet another process, one well worth the effort. I believe I am happy; I search for evidence to support this belief; when I find such evidence, I reinforce the belief. It's a positive cycle that begins with the belief. I must "claim it, then live it." I must learn to believe it can be true. Sometimes I must ignore setbacks and just keep moving ahead with faith—believing it is possible—in order to make progress. I did not become happy, joyous, and free overnight—it took me a couple of years to succeed at maintaining happiness. I did not become happy, joyous, and free in some sequential order. My days did not get progressively happier; the length of my happiness did not grow longer as time went by. Some days I could see no progress at all. Sometimes I was depressed, but I kept believing and looking for evidence of my happiness. I kept finding this evidence, too. As time went by, I became happy, joyous, and free. Persistence paid off big time! These days, being "happy, joyous, and free" is second nature. I do not work for it; I just am. I believe it!

Since, like most people, I tend to gather information to support my dominant beliefs, it is important to identify what those beliefs are. If I know what my beliefs are, I can better support them. On the contrary, I may discover I hold beliefs I no longer wish to have, let alone support. This search for dominant beliefs is critical if I am interested in changing who I am because, as I discovered, my beliefs dictate my actions.

Just how do I go about defining my beliefs? Well, I found this to be a little tricky at first. I started out by writing down what I believed. This did not work out very well because, at first, I didn't know for sure what I believed. I used to spend so much time believing I would have another beer. I pretty much let everything else come and go as it pleased. Still, I wrote what I could, and I thought a lot. I wrote some more, although in the end I had written very little. Then an idea struck me.

I can do this, I thought, by observing my actions and by watching the information I gather to see what beliefs it supports. Instead of taking a belief and supporting it, I would watch to see what I was supporting with evidence I would gather by monitoring my action. Using this process—a tedious one, but one that has worked—I can determine what I believe. Since I was already watching my thoughts, I reasoned, why not use the information I gathered to identify my beliefs? I can then check with my sponsor and trusted friends to see if my beliefs are steering me wrong. If my beliefs are solid, I can go on supporting them. If they are causing me difficulty, then I can do something different.

When I find that I hold a belief I do not like, I can change that belief. Here is a fun situation, because I did not previously believe that I could. How do you change a belief just like that? Well, I didn't do it "just like that"; I did it over time. I once believed that I had to drink, but I no longer believe this to be true. So I had changed a belief I had held for a long time. This one fact gave me the boost I needed to begin looking at how I might be able to change any belief I held that I found to be detrimental to my happiness and well-being. As I was pondering this fact, I decided that I could change any belief I held. As I moved forward in this area, I discovered updating my beliefs to be essential.

Updating my beliefs is necessary because I am constantly changing. I am different today than I was yesterday. I may be only a little different, yet I am much different than I was six months ago; the longer the time period, the more I have changed. I had to update my beliefs regarding my drinking and many other areas of my life. I will continue to update what I believe for as long as I live. Life is a process, a series of changes; these changes require me to continue to update my belief system. In fact, as life changes, as I change, I learn to see things differently. Because I see things differently, my beliefs change whether I notice the change or not. By noticing the beliefs I hold, I can learn to support the ones I find beneficial and discard the ones that hold me back. In this way, I can grow in the direction I choose instead of allowing faulty thinking and beliefs—or other people, places, or things—to dictate what direction I take with my life.

Using the Serenity Prayer, I ask for courage to change the things I can, and for the most part I can really only change myself. By taking control of my beliefs, I take control of who I am. Isn't that why I quit drinking—so I could get some control over my life?

While this was at first a difficult and time-consuming process, it has become easier with practice. Time marches on whether I make the effort or not. The choice is mine. As I mentioned earlier, because I have made the effort, it has simply become a part of who I am. It has become second nature to update my belief system, just as it has become second nature to monitor my thoughts. I still make mistakes. I still have instances when I doubt myself. Some thoughts slip through no matter how hard I try to watch them all. I still have times of sadness, when I am not "happy, joyous, and free." Life happens, and life for me today is not about being perfect; it is about making progress. Today, I am all about the progress.

TODAY I DO MY BEST TO SEE

FAILURE IN A DIFFERENT

LIGHT. I SEE IT AS AN

OPPORTUNITY, SO IT DOES

NOT CONCERN ME AS MUCH

WHEN IT HAPPENS BECAUSE

FAILURE *IS* AN OPTION.

IT HAPPENS. SOMETIMES

IT HAPPENS NO MATTER HOW

WELL I PLAN, HOW MUCH

HELP I ASK FOR, OR HOW

MUCH HELP I RECEIVE.

6

PERFECTION AND PERFECTIONISM

I have had to learn to live within the scope of my limited abilities. When I was younger, I believed I could do anything—especially when I was drinking. I thought I was "ten feet tall and bulletproof," but I also thought I had to do everything "right." I held a deep belief that making a mistake was avoidable. I believed I *should* avoid mistakes at all costs. Mistakes were failures, and failures were the end of success—the beginning of humiliation. I had to be perfect at everything I tried, even if it was my first try at something new. I believed I had to do my absolute best to achieve perfection.

As a child, I remember receiving a model airplane as a birthday gift. I do not remember exactly what kind of plane it was supposed to be when it was put together; I do know it was a complicated build, a B-29 or some such thing. That unbuilt model sat on my closet shelf for a very long time because I was not very good at building models (I knew this from previous attempts) and the thought of building something so complicated drove me crazy. As I realize now, another reason I left it alone for so long was because I did want to try to build it. I just wanted everyone else to forget I had it in case I failed. If I failed, I could throw it away and nobody would be the wiser. I know this because, as it turned out, I did fail, and I did throw it away; then I had to lie about it when my brother—who is a wonderful model builder—asked me if I wanted some help putting it together. In a panic, I said I would "go look for it." Of course, I could not find it because I was looking in my closet, while it was long gone with the trash.

I had help available—my brother—and still I did not ask for help. What's up with that? Today, I realize perfectionism kept me from asking for help. Perfectionism tells me I am supposed to be able to do things perfectly the first time and without help. Perfectionism is a great liar. It somehow convinces me to believe that which flies in the face of pretty much everything I have learned through experience to be true. I will need help and I will make mistakes. If I had asked for my brother's help, I could have ended up with a cool model. I would have also gained some model-building skills by learning from someone who knew models and enjoyed building them. Instead I listened to perfectionism, which told me to go it alone, fail, and then try to cover up the mistake. What a waste of time, energy, effort, and a cool model.

Yes, I must learn to live within my limited abilities. However, I must remember they are abilities, not disabilities. Even the things I am not good at doing, or do not know how to do, are not disabilities—they are opportunities to learn. There are a few things I have a penchant for in life. It is no coincidence these are the same things I am good at. I have been practicing them for some time. I enjoy computers. I am not as good with computers as I once was because the technology has moved ahead very rapidly and I have not kept up. However, if you ask any of my friends, they will tell you I am a computer whiz. I can attribute their rather high opinion of me to two things. First, they know very little about computers, which makes what I know look impressive. Even though it pales in comparison to what there is to know in the field, what I know about and am able to do with computers is well beyond what many people comprehend. The second and much more important attributing factor is that I have been playing around with computers for twenty-five years.

My first computer was an Apple IIe, which I got in 1983 and still own today. While I do not use it anymore, I keep it around. I do keep threatening to break it out to play some of the classic games I have for it. It reminds me of the way computers used to be. It has sentimental value. The point I am trying to make is that I do have abilities, and not just with computers. You do, too. It can help to write down all the things you are good at doing. Be generous, too. Cleaning house counts, as do cooking, changing the oil in a car, yard work, your job; the list could be much longer than you might expect. We all have abilities we use every day, yet we give ourselves very little credit for using them. Instead, we tend to focus on what we cannot do by ourselves. I am trying to break this habit.

I am doing my best to break away from thinking I have to be perfect, thinking I am perfect, or even trying to be perfect. In fact, I am taking things to a new level, as I like to do, by admitting I need help. I am asking for help when I think I can use it—not when I need it. By the time I decide I "need" help, things have become messy from my attempt to "go it alone." I am embarrassed by the havoc I have created, and my helper has anywhere from two to a hundred times more work to do to bail me out than they would have had if I had asked before I attempted to do something that I knew was out of my league.

Today I think things through to determine if I have the ability to accomplish the task. I get honest with myself, and then I answer. I am often humbled with an answer of "No, you will need help with this," but today I can take that in stride. I remember that I have strong abilities, just not in every area. I see asking for help as an opportunity to learn. I do my best to look forward to the possibility of adding a new ability to my list by asking for help, and then assisting, or at least watching, the person I have asked for help while they are working. I even ask questions in order to learn as much as I can during the process of accomplishing the task for which I have asked for help. Finally, I have found that, for the most part, people love to teach as much as they love to help.

I have come to believe—through participating in and watching what happens during the process of asking for help—that having limits on my abilities is actually a good thing. If I were perfect, I would need no one else in my life; there would be no challenges, and things would get very boring because I would not be able to "put myself to the test," so to speak. If I were perfect, I could isolate, and isolating is not what human beings do. We are social creatures. As much as I have come to enjoy my time alone, I still need to interact with other people in order to fulfill a basic need, which seems built-in to all humans. My limited abilities keep me in touch with the world around me. While I see my limits today as a good thing, I have come to realize that no matter how many abilities I do acquire, there are certain things I will never be able to do alone, and for a variety of reasons. Whether it is because of time constraints—I am a busy person—or the fact I do not possess the skills required, or merely because the world is such a large place, I will always have limits. I need to see my limits as opportunities to learn and grow. I need to use the tools that are available to me in order to make the most of the abilities I do have.

By myself I cannot tell what is happening around the world, but with the help of the media—television, newspapers, magazines, and the Internet—I am able to keep up with current events. I use this help all the time. I use many forms of help, without much thought. Without my car I would have trouble getting to work, or to a meeting; without my computer, I would have much more difficulty writing. Without farmers and grocery stores, I would starve to death. All of this help comes in the form of distant human interaction. The people involved are vague acquaintances at best, unknown completely in most instances, and in some cases the tools I use are machines, like my car—although I know they were built by other people. I seem to have little trouble asking these machines, vague acquaintances, and unknown people for their help, but when it comes to asking for direct help, things become more difficult. I do not understand why this is so; I only know it is a truth in my life. I also know I dislike it. Therefore, I am practicing asking for help when I think I can use it, because it helps me to ward off the persistence of perfectionism.

Perfectionism is a subtle foe, and a confusing one, too. It tells me I must be able to do things right the first time I make an attempt, while at the same time telling me I will most likely fail. At the same time it tells me failure is not an option, it reminds me not to ask for help. Perfectionism fills me with fear. There is the fear of not being good enough to do it by myself, and the fear of failure. These are all wrapped up in a neat little package that is so cute that I can hardly resist the temptation to open it to see what is inside. Perfectionism tells me that asking for help is failure. It also tells me failure is the end of the line. To perfectionism, I am learning to say, "Hogwash."

I decided that in order to put perfectionism in its place, I must admit I am human and learn to allow myself to fail—and even enjoy failing. This was a perplexing concept at first. It took me a while to even conclude that it might be a beneficial path to follow. Perfectionism sat on my shoulder, whispering to me not to proceed because it would not work. "You will fail and you will not like it at all," Perfectionism snidely proclaimed. "You will fail and that will be the end of another wasted attempt." This turned out to be just what I needed to hear to get me going. I learned Perfectionism was a liar, that what I was told must not be true, and if it was not true, maybe the opposite was true. Maybe it would work; maybe I could learn to enjoy failing. It did seem a stretch, but I figured I had little to lose, so I made a go of it.

While I must admit that I have not yet reached the point where I actually do enjoy failing, I fear it much less, and I no longer see failure as an end. I see failure as a beginning. Since I like beginnings—I have always been intrigued with starting things, although finishing has been difficult for me—I began to see failure as something of a good thing. Therefore, I like failure. It still sounds strange to say it like that, but it is not such a producer of fear for me anymore. As I practice having courage enough to fail, as I also practice seeing failure as a beginning. I see some of the good that comes from failure.

Many good things come from failure. Learning is a good example. There are lessons to be learned when I fail. If I am paying attention, I can reap wonderful rewards from a failure. I can almost certainly learn what not to do next time. I can often learn what to do next time as well. I usually do not learn from my successes. They tend to support my current thought processes and beliefs. While success usually feels good in the short term, it gives strength to Perfectionism. Perfectionism feeds on my successes. When I succeed, Perfectionism tells me I do not need help.

While failure is not a bed of roses, it isn't a bed of thorns, either. Failure hurts; there's no arguing that point. Failing at something causes me to look bad, costs me money, slaps my ego, and even hurts my family and friends sometimes. However, failure also encourages me to ask for help next time, keeps me in touch with people, teaches me lessons (some I wish I had already learned), and provides me with new opportunities to learn and grow. Now that I have a better working "thinker," I do my best to think my way through a situation to see if I might need help. I do this before I make an attempt and I do it honestly. I have done my best to turn what fear of failure I still have into an ally. This keeps me honest and allows me to understand that I might require help with some things in life. If I can put away my denial and seek the truth, I will find just how much help I take for granted. I will discover that I am not a burden on others for asking for help, and I will find that failure is an option.

Yes, failure is an option. I may not directly choose to fail; I may fail simply by not asking for help, by asking for the wrong help, or by not planning well enough to know of all the help I will need. These are choices I made that led me to failure before. I am certain they will visit me again in days to come. However, today I do my best to see failure in a different light. I see it as an opportunity, so it does not concern me as much when it happens because failure *is* an option. It happens. Sometimes it happens no matter how well I plan, how much help I ask for, or how much help I receive.

Sometimes I simply cannot see everything that might "go wrong" with a situation or project. In these cases, failure of some kind is imminent. It is not a matter of if I will fail. It is a matter of how bad things will get before I and my helpers can figure out what to do to correct the matter. Regardless of what I do in life, I will have failures. If I can stop seeing them as an end and start to see them as beginnings, I will be better able to endure the difficulties that will inevitably come my way.

When I fail, I usually see that I will need help in correcting the situation. If I had a dollar for every time I had to have someone bail me out of a tough situation I had created for myself, I would have a bundle of dollars, to be sure. I should not wait until I need bailing out in order to ask for help. Life is a process, and I am learning all the time. Today, my goal is not to know everything. My goal is to know when to ask for help so I will ask before I need bailing out. I am sure I will not figure this out anytime soon. I still like to do things myself. Sometimes I like to try something to see if I can do it on my own. When I do, I find it important to admit that I can't do it and surrender to the fact that I have taken on a task that is way over my head. All that has really happened is that I have tried to push my boundaries and have found my limits before I was able to complete the project. At this point, I can ask for help in completing the project and stretching my boundaries. This is part of the process of life. It is also part of why failure is inevitable.

I have to push myself in order to grow. I must test my boundaries in order to see where they really are, as opposed to where I think they might be. The key is to take my time with this process. My first sponsor liked to tell me, "Don't try to get too good by Thursday." The first time he said it, I had no clue as to what he meant. It is a way to help me slow down; I need to remember that no matter how hard I try, I cannot do everything today. Some things must wait for another day. Life is a process, and sometimes it is better to let it unfold than to chase after it. I needed a little patience. "Don't try to get too good by Thursday" reminds me that I have more than a week to live the rest of my life. It also reminds me to let the process of life take its time.

"Don't try to get too good by Thursday" also reminds me that I will have failures as I move along in life. What I am learning to like about failure is that it is a teacher. Pain, on the other hand, is not. I have suffered many failures in my life, and looking back, I can find lessons in every one of them. I have also suffered great pain in this life—physical, mental, emotional, social, and spiritual pain. However, I have learned very little from pain. Even though pain generally hurts far more than failure—in fact, it is not the failure that actually hurts, it is the pain of humiliation that hurts—pain, for me, is not much of a teacher. Avoiding pain may motivate, but it does not teach me. Pain simply points me in a new direction—sometimes to the hospital! Yet I must move on my own or call for help. It is I who must learn and then practice new behavior.

Now that I know pain and failure are not the same thing, I can separate the two. While I know pain is sometimes caused by failure, I also know neither one will kill me. In fact, I have failed enough times in my life—and I am not dead yet—to see that failure is not the end of life. It is the beginning of a learning opportunity. Through failing and learning, I can make progress; that progress is the real goal.

Spiritual progress and not spiritual perfection has a deep meaning for me. Spiritual progress comes from failure, followed by pain, followed by a new direction. Failure is part of the process I must go through in order to grow spiritually. Failure is also part of the process I must go through in order to grow mentally, emotionally, socially, and physically. I must learn that even though I will most likely always fear failure, I can put that fear to good use. I can use it to help me plan properly, to keep myself honest about my abilities, and to ask for help when I think I could use it to obtain a goal. Once I am able to use this fear of failure properly, I can make progress in finding proper practices for growth that will lead to fewer failures and more growth. The greatest of these practices is to ask for help when I think it will be beneficial.

My mother used to tell me, "You should learn from other people's mistakes; you will not live long enough to make them all yourself." Much wisdom is within this statement, and it goes in the opposite direction as well. I must learn from other people's successes too, for I will not live long enough to figure out everything on my own. By listening to others, I can learn from their failures and their successes. I have found this to be one of the greatest advantages of attending meetings. People share honestly about what has worked and what has not worked in their lives. From these stories I can learn new practices to exercise in my life—ones that will help me to become a better person.

Practice makes progress, not perfection. Even through practice, I will not become perfect. However, with practice I can become better at doing things well. In fact, through practice I have become good at the things I already do well. (I used to practice drinking and I got pretty good at it, especially if you consider consuming large quantities of alcohol as being "good at drinking.") Today, I practice other things—recovery things. Over time, I am getting better at the sober things in life. I am becoming a better person through practice.

Just as a fishhook has many fish swimming around it, yet catches only one, I may not catch everything the first time. Still, I do seem to catch what I need when I need it if I am paying attention. Once I catch something, I can go back for more. If I choose to see not catching all the fish my first time around as a failure, then I magnify the impact failure has on my life. However, if I can see that I do not have to get too good by, say, Thursday, then I learn that I can go back for more fish later. When I catch only one fish, it is a success, and I can begin to see my growth.

By changing my attitude about what failure is and how I will let it affect me, I can change how I behave in matters I deem to be difficult. Sure, I may fail the first time I attempt something new, but if I can see failure as an opportunity to learn and begin again, I stand a greater chance of changing my attitude about a lot more than just how I see failure. I can change how I see the world, and I can change my part in it as well. In the process of growth, I work on being less judgmental of myself and of others. I am learning to see "failure" as a beginning and not the end.

IN ORDER TO LOVE WHO I AM

TODAY, I MUST ACCEPT MY

PAST, BECAUSE IT HAS MADE

ME WHO I AM. IF IT WERE NOT

FOR MY PAST, THERE WOULD

BE NO ME IN THE HERE AND

NOW. I AM EXACTLY WHO AND

WHERE I AM TODAY BECAUSE

OF WHO I USED TO BE AND

WHAT I HAVE DONE.

7

JUDGING/GUILT AND CHARACTER DEFECTS

Judge, jury, and executioner—these were roles I played every day. Even after I had been in recovery a while, I found it second nature to judge other people. I judged their behavior against what they said. I judged their actions in general. I thought I could tell who would and would not maintain long-term recovery just by the way they acted in rehab, and when I got out of rehab, I could tell by how they acted in meetings. I watched people with a careful eye because I wanted to keep score so I could stay in the lead, or at least in the "top tier." I still wanted to be the best—even if it meant being the best rehab client, which might mean being the worst. My habit of judging other people was so deeply ingrained that I rarely knew when I was judging, or if I was judging, let alone by what rules.

As it turns out, judging is heavy work, and while I cannot say that I no longer judge people, I can say I have made tremendous progress in this area. It has not been easy to give up judging and condemning, but I do my best these days to leave it to God to decide who is good and who is bad. I do my best just to see people being people. The road has been a long one, and there is more traveling to do in my journey to be less judgmental; however, I find the less time I spend judging people, the freer I am to be me. The steps helped me find this freedom.

When I did my fourth step and wrote my moral inventory, I discovered I had done many things that embarrassed me, hurt me and those around me, and generally gave me reason to believe that I was worthy of judgment in the harshest manner by the "court" in my head. The court was composed of judge, jury, and executioner— my inner voices, with which I have an ongoing and usually negative dialog. My inventory was so bad—I thought— that a drink might be required to wash away the pain. I called my sponsor. We talked briefly. Then I asked him if he was ready for me to do my fifth step. His reply was: "The real question is, are you ready to do a fifth step?" Yes, I was. In addition to realizing it was a necessary element of the program for my recovery, I figured getting this stuff out in the open, and getting his opinion on what kind of person I was, might help me get off my own case. I drove to my sponsor's house and we went through my list, item by item. I bared my soul, sharing with him every twisted thing I had ever done. Although I wanted to keep many things to myself, I held nothing back, because I knew I had to be rigorously honest—Steps Four and Five required it. Looking back, I see it does not matter how I motivated myself to do the fifth step; it only matters that I did one. I did it for immediate release. I received much more, but it did begin with a kind of emotional release. In many ways it felt as though a burden had been lifted from my shoulders; yet initially I felt ashamed.

When I had finished with my monologue—which my sponsor sat through without saying a word—I was feeling like the lowest form of scum on the planet. The "judge" had passed sentence in my head, and I was going away for a long time. I fell silent, having given the final testimony against myself, and looked at my sponsor. He sat quietly in his seat, eyes closed, for so long that I began to think he had fallen asleep, even though he was sitting in his studious posture, hands folded, index fingers pointed up and touching his lower lip, and his head bowed ever-so-slightly forward even though his body was reclining in the chair. I waited for him to tell me what a horrible person I was. Then I waited for him to say anything. Just as I began to wonder if he had really fallen asleep on me during my most trying hour, he spoke.

"Is that all you have?" he asked, as though there should be more. I panicked and looked at my list. I had left nothing out; I had nothing more to offer.

"Yes that's it," I replied, suddenly thinking, "I have bared my soul here!" Here I've just dumped all my garbage, and he asks, "Is that all you have?" Indignation set in; I began to wonder if he had been sleeping after all. "Is that all you have?" seemed an insult. I had laid the horror of my life at his feet for judgment. Just as I was beginning to work myself into a frenzy, he spoke again.

"I have heard worse things from priests," he said as he opened his eyes and looked at me for the first time in maybe an hour. His look floored me as much as his words.

While I did not know exactly what to do with the words, the look conveyed love and compassion. This was something I had not been expecting—actually, two somethings I had not been expecting.

I had expected to be judged harshly, yet I was not. I had expected him to shun me for the lack of discernment I had shown in the past. He did neither, at least not with his actions. He had heard worse things from priests? What was he saying? Was I better than a priest? No! That was not possible. There are priests who are much better people than I am. Finally, some kind of meaning came ringing home. I am better than some priests. This was possible in my limited and judgmental world, so I accepted it, sat back, and tried to relax for a moment. I had completed my confession; my Fifth Step was over. I noticed I was sweating slightly.

"Let's go have some pie," my sponsor announced as he began to rise from his chair. "Pie is always good, especially so when shared amongst friends." We went into the kitchen and had pie. We talked about the weather and other superficial things for a while. This very casual conversation went on for maybe half an hour. Nothing serious was mentioned, for reasons I still could not put my finger on—although maybe no finger needs to be put on it—when finally I began to realize he still cared about me. He had called me his friend after I had told on myself. None of the bad things I had done seemed to matter to him. When I could take it no longer, I opened my mouth and changed the subject from superficial to serious.

"I poured out my soul. I told you every bad thing I have ever done. All you had to say was you had heard worse from priests. How can that be?" Without hesitation, he replied, "I worked with priests for years, did you forget that? I worked third shift, too. When they could not sleep, they would come and talk with me. I did the equivalent of a Fifth Step with priests on hundreds of occasions."

It came back to me that he had worked in a treatment facility for priests. He had told me this. He was not making it up or exaggerating. He really had heard worse from priests. I had some thinking to do. Fortunately for me, my sponsor could read me like a book. He told me to go home and think on what had transpired that day. "Think real hard on it and call me tomorrow," he said. I told him I would, and then he threw in, "Thank God. Carefully read Steps One through Five of the Twelve Steps and ask if you have forgotten anything. A solid foundation is essential if you are to be free of your past and to experience the freedom of a new life." I promised I would, and I left for home.

When I arrived at home, I began to feel the immediate release for which I had been hoping. I began to feel as though the tonnage of my past was being blasted away, bits at a time. This was a wonderful feeling; however, it was nothing compared to the revelation that my sponsor still cared about me even though I had been such a horrible person. I reviewed Steps One through Five as he'd recommended, and decided I had left nothing out. I was satisfied with the work I had done so far. I read Steps Six and Seven—pondering them for a while. After deciding I was ready for the next two steps, I took a break, and for the rest of the day I relaxed the best I could.

It was in doing Step Six that I began to discover just how foolish I had been in judging people. I discovered in my working of Step Six that I have had a difficult time determining my own positive and negative traits. When working Steps Six and Seven, I tried to write down my character defects. Then I tried to fix them instead of asking God to remove them. Finally, when things were not working out for me, I did turn it over to God. That is when I discovered He could use my defects for doing good. This is also how I discovered that I was a poor judge of what is good and bad when it comes to judging myself as well as others.

A partial list of my character defects included fear, anger, resentment, dishonesty, procrastination, inflated ego, false pride, guilt, impatience, denial, jealousy, envy, laziness, negative thinking, perfectionism, gossip, and high expectations. (Defects are listed in no particular order, and this is not a complete list—the original is much longer— but it will suffice to show that these characteristics are not all bad.) While they may seem bad on the surface, I have learned these character "defects" are not all bad.

FEAR

Fear can keep me from doing things I would like to do. Fear brought about misfortune and misery, and I had to realize I was responsible for much of my fear. Fear, in and of itself, is nothing more than a feeling, or emotion, and if I pay attention to fear it may tell me things I need to know—like something is wrong or out of place; maybe even I am wrong or out of place. While fear may try to make me do stupid things, it does not act for me. Fear is a warning signal, and, last I knew, warning signals were a good thing—like the ones at railroad crossings, or tornado warnings, which can help me avoid disaster. I am sure you can easily recall a whole slew of bad things to say about fear, and I would not argue. Some fears are bad—useless and destructive. However, having fear is not, in-and-of-itself a bad thing. Fear can be used for good, and God can teach me how to do so if I listen and watch for His help. Most of the destructive fear I have today comes in two forms: fear of losing something I already have, and fear of not getting something I desperately want. I believe these are the most destructive forms of fear, because they can cause me to do unwise things in order to obtain and keep things, things I believe I need but that I may actually not need. I may actually be better off without them. Sometimes God allows me to lose one thing so He can replace it with another, and better yet, He replaces it with things I can use. So I ask myself—why do I fear loss?

When I am feeling fearful, I find it most important to ask myself why. Why am I feeling fear? It can sometimes take a lot of soul-searching to discover the truth, but if I am willing to go through with the work of figuring out what is wrong, I will be better able to find a plan of corrective action.

ANGER AND RESENTMENT

Like fear, anger and resentment are warning signals that something is wrong. Often, what's wrong is what's wrong with me. No one else can make me feel angry. People do things all the time that I choose to be angry about, but nobody has ever made me angry, just as no one has ever made me happy.

Doing away with anger and resentment can and indeed should be a top priority. This is a tall order; however, it is possible. Again, progress, and not perfection, is the goal. I have nearly rid myself of anger and resentment through the practice of remembering it is my choice to be angry or happy, resentful or forgiving. This realization is an uphill climb in the beginning, but it is a trip worth taking—the peace of mind is amazing.

The most stunning thing I have found about anger is that when I am most angry is when I am most wrong. I usually get mad when I am wrong and someone shows me the truth of the situation. The further from that truth I am, the madder I get.

Certainly not all my anger comes from my being wrong. Other people make mistakes, too. This is where my resentments come from for the most part, and where forgiveness can take me a long way toward recovery. Instead of judging other people—determining they are out to get me, or some such thing—I can give them the benefit of the doubt that I would like to be granted if I had made the blunder. If I am willing to put myself in their shoes for just a moment, ask myself what I could use at that particular moment, I would most likely wish for some form of clemency. Therefore, I have found it best to grant the same clemency I would wish for to others when they make an error. We all make mistakes. It is about time I stopped taking the mistakes of others so personally. The whole world is not out to get me, regardless what my belief may tell me.

DISHONESTY

I have yet to find anything good about dishonesty in any form. Dishonesty does not just mean lying. It also means a lack of integrity. Lacking honesty and integrity is something I have had an impossible time finding anything good to say about, so you might wonder why I use dishonesty as an example here. Truth is, so do I. Maybe it is because some things are just plain wrong. However, I have learned something about honesty from my past dishonesty, which is to say that I can be honest without hurting other people. I do not have to be dishonest to save someone from hurt feelings.

The best example I know of with regard to being honest, to myself as well as to others, without hurting myself or others, is that I have learned I do not have to give full disclosure at all times. In fact, full disclosure is often simply a form of excuse, and my excuses are for me, not for the other person. If invited to a party and I do not want to go, I can simply say, "I have other plans." I do not have to elaborate; I do not have to give details of my plans. My "other plans" might include sitting at home reading a book. Odds are, the person who invited me to the party is not going to see my reason as good enough to not attend the party, but it is a good enough reason as far as I am concerned, and that is what counts. Therefore, I can keep the actual reason for my not attending to myself. This is my understanding of integrity. I decline the invitation. I am true to myself, without causing undue harm to the person who was kind enough to ask me to join them.

I give this example in order to show how important it can be to use caution when it comes to all of my "character defects." I must look for the middle of the path when it comes to how all of these characteristics are used. While I should not lean to one extreme, I should also avoid the other.

PROCRASTINATION

Procrastination is something I used to think of as nothing more or less than evil. Today, I see things differently. Putting things off can be a good thing on occasion. A prime example occurs when I am driving down the road and someone pulls out in front of me. If I can procrastinate long enough on my temptation to give them an undesirable hand gesture,

I will most likely come to realize it would only have made things worse if I had chosen not to procrastinate. Biting my tongue is another positive form of procrastination. Not saying hurtful things is a wonderful form of procrastinating; I usually find putting it off leads to not saying them at all.

My favorite type of procrastination comes in a form that was new to me when I joined the ranks of the recovering; I learned it from my first sponsor. (I may have heard it before this, but he brought it home to me as a positive lesson, one I do my best to follow.) He told me:

"If you don't know what to do, don't do anything."

This is a positive form of procrastination, in that it involves putting something off, meaning I am taking no action now. However, I am doing so with good reason. I don't know what to do; therefore, anything I actually do could make things worse. The truth is, if I do nothing for a while, the situation will change for better or worse and I will come to know what action to take. Through this exercise, I have found that doing nothing is a form of doing something. Sometimes it is right and proper to procrastinate and sometimes it is not. Again, it is up to me to find the middle ground: the right path to take, the proper action— or inaction.

INFLATED EGO

Inflated ego is a slippery beast. I like to feel good about myself. Here again, it is the middle ground I am looking for. An overinflated ego is usually nothing but trouble, yet from a properly inflated ego comes confidence. Like a tire on a car, over- or underinflation is not appropriate; either an over- or an underinflated ego can send me into the ditch. The important thing for me to remember is that confidence comes from my ego, and confidence is required, at least to some extent, in order for me to function—especially under pressure. For this reason, I must check my ego inflation occasionally to make sure it is proper, neither too low nor too high.

FALSE PRIDE

Self-deprecation can be a sign of false pride. When people praise me and I tell them "it was nothing," or that I did not do anything important, or my part was nonexistent, I'm not only telling them they're wrong, I'm subtly stroking my own ego. I did not understand what I was doing until a friend of mine told me I needed to learn to "say thank you, then shut up." He pointed out that denial of my part in any good outcome was nothing more than a plea for more attention. While that was a confusing concept at first, I came to see the truth of the matter.

When someone praises me for a job well done, and I refuse the compliment by saying something similar to "Ah, shucks, it was nothing," this encourages them to repeat the compliment, and usually they will, sometimes more strenuously. They might come back with "Yes it was, you worked hard to make that happen, and you deserve a lot of credit." This can actually go on for some time, until I simply say thank you (and then shut up), or until the other person gets tired of repeating the same compliment.

While false pride is not a good thing, I do need to have some pride in the things I do and the accomplishments I have made. When I look back over the years I have been sober, I see many achievements worthy of praise, and when someone wishes to commend me on my successes today, I say thank you; then I shut up. Then I thank God for both the achievement and the ability to accept praise with grace.

GUILT

Guilt is not just a character defect, but rather, it is a tool. Guilt tells me when I have gone against my better thinking and beliefs. Guilt tells me when I have wronged myself, and possibly others. While I refuse to sit around and kick myself over things today, I do see feeling guilty as a necessary tool for improvement. I do have a new attitude toward guilt these days. I allow myself one swift kick in the rear end for the improper behavior. I then do my best to learn from the mistake and move on. If I notice another desire to kick myself, I simply remind myself I have done that already. I will not need another, for I have learned my lesson. I move on.

IMPATIENCE

Impatience is a tough one. I wanted my impatience removed immediately, as do most of us, and I wanted it done without any discomfort or sacrifice. What I found, though, was that impatience removed itself as I practiced the things I had learned about my other defects. These things take time. Everything takes time. Some things take longer than others do, yet it seems most things take longer than I would like. But I must remember, time too shall pass, and all things will happen when they are supposed to, not when I want them to. I have actually found it best to deal with my impatience by dealing with my other defects—waiting for progress, and then seeing the results.

Seeing delayed gratification for what it is can be very beneficial. While my tendency is to look for instant gratification, I do my best now to look for instant gratitude. Still, impatience can lead me to work harder for the things I desire. As long as I am working toward admirable goals,

I can use my impatience to drive me. It helps me to focus my effort. It is always wise to find a little acceptance for the current situation.

DENIAL

Denial can be useful in helping me deal with my impatience. I can learn to deny that I need things to be different. I used to do it all the time when I refused to believe I should quit drinking. Why should I not use it now in order to appease my impatience? Denial is not always bad. It is usually worse when I use it to deny that things should be as they are, or to deny there is a problem that needs attention, or to tell myself things that are just not true. I can use denial properly if I put away my dishonesty and reach for the truth.

JEALOUSY AND ENVY

Jealousy and envy are the green-eyed monsters. I have found these emotions to be undesirable, yet if I see something or somebody I envy, I can use the envy to drive myself toward achievement. It is important to remember that it will take time and effort. I must accept things as they are for now. However, I can use jealousy and envy to make myself a better person if they prompt me to work harder for the things I desire.

LAZINESS

Laziness can help me relax; however, it's often misunderstood. I need to recharge my batteries, so to speak, in order to be at my top performance. I can use my laziness to aid me in relaxing and recharging myself as long as I do not let guilt get in the way. One very important consideration is to be honest about whether I am being lazy or I am relaxing. If I am relaxing, I need to allow myself to do so. Even just being lazy can be fun, as long as I allow it and do not feel guilty. While being lazy can be hurtful, it can also be a path to serenity. I need to have a more relaxed attitude about life, and a little laziness can help me find this road if I allow it to.

NEGATIVE THINKING AND PERFECTIONISM

Negative thinking and perfectionism are both character defects I have recognized in myself, so they are listed here; however, they have been dealt with elsewhere in this book.

HIGH EXPECTATIONS

Having high expectations can be a defect of character. I can hold others to impossible standards, and I can do the same thing to myself. Paradoxically, though, without reaching beyond my grasp, I grow very little. Without expecting much of others, I will never help them achieve more for themselves, either. I have found high expectations to be crucial to my growth at times. The way I temper my expectations is through acceptance. I can expect anything from myself or others as long as I am willing to accept whatever happens.

I am currently in school again after many years away, and I am carrying a very high grade point average. I have come to expect I will maintain this grade point average. In fact, I fully expect it to happen until I attain my degree. If, for some reason, I should receive a grade less than what I have come to expect, I would need to accept that fact in order to move on. These are high expectations tempered with acceptance.

GOSSIP

Gossip is a funny thing. I think I am talking about other people when I gossip, but I am actually talking about myself. My first sponsor once told me, "There is no gossip in this program." I laughed. He did not laugh; he simply continued. "All people are doing is taking their own inventory and putting someone else's name on it." While I would love to tell you this has cured me of gossip, I regret to inform you it has not. I do know what I am doing when I am gossiping now. This helps me to limit my gossip.

JUDGING (AGAIN)

It was confusing, at first, to understand how God could use my defects for doing good; however, the harder I looked, the more I saw it was true. I found through various sources that the defects I possessed could be useful. As I sought the truth about myself, it was revealed—sometimes more slowly than I would have liked, but always it came. When the truth became evident, I did my best to practice the new lessons I learned until they became habit. I changed who I was consciously; I no longer simply "went along for the ride." Still, there were a few important lessons about judging that I needed to learn.

It is very difficult for me to tell what characteristics might be good or bad for another person. If I cannot tell what are character defects for me, how could I possibly know what another person might need, or be defective or deficient in? Gradually I am becoming less judgmental, and possibly the greatest lesson of all is that "just because I do not like something, it is not bad or wrong *per se*." I have often judged an event in my past to be the worst thing that could have possibly happened to me. Only later did

I discover that it was the best thing that ever happened to me—like quitting drinking and drugging.

"If I were you, him, her, or them . . . I would . . ." This is always faulty thinking for me, because I rarely know, with absolute certainty, what I would or would not do in a given situation. Unless I have been in another person's shoes, it is impossible for me to tell what I might do. Even if I were in a similar situation, I would most likely not do the exact thing I say I would do beforehand. I can think of times when I have looked at a friend and said to myself, "He should dump that girlfriend, she treats him so poorly." Taking an honest look back at my own relationships, I see that I have put up with treatment from some women that could be considered far worse than the treatment my friend was receiving, and which I was judging so harshly.

I have found it beneficial to simply stop trying to decide what I might do if some particular thing happens. I do my best to heed the advice my first sponsor gave me when he said, "Don't make up your mind about things that haven't happened yet."

I am finding it hard enough to make up my mind about things that are happening or have already happened without worrying about what might happen in the future. I know I should avoid this form of worry. If I delay making up my mind about things that have not yet happened, I accomplish two goals: I free my mind to work in the present, and I release myself from possible self-judgment for not doing what I said or thought I would do if and when I might find myself in those situations. A third benefit of waiting is that I find myself becoming less judgmental of the way others handle situations.

To become less judgmental of others and myself, I have found it important to become more forgiving. It is extremely difficult to be judgmental of others after they have been forgiven, or even as I am trying to forgive them. Forgiveness comes rather easily when I look at it properly, although in some cases it can be a difficult process. When we feel we have been wronged, it can take some work before we forgive. Yet, when I remember to forgive someone—not for their sake, but for mine—it makes forgiving myself much easier. While I have found it a tough sell at times to convince myself that I am forgiving someone for my own good, especially when I consider their conduct to be grievous, I have found it to be true. In fact, in cases where I have considered someone's actions to be atrocious, I have found this truth to be most evident. It seems, from my experience, that the worse I consider the act against me, the more benefit I gain from forgiveness. This forgiveness applies to offenses against myself and against others.

Guilt is a form of judgment against myself. It seems when it comes to my own misbehavior, I almost enjoy being judge, jury, and executioner—especially executioner. I can kick myself for days, even weeks, over the smallest misstep. Because of this tendency to beat myself up, I revert to the one-kick rule mentioned earlier. When I make a mistake, I allow myself one swift kick in the rear. Then I do my absolute best to learn what lesson needs learning, and to move on. If I find myself wanting to do some more kicking, I simply remind myself that I have already punished myself for that action; I have paid my dues. Then I do what I can to correct the situation. If I am unable to correct the situation, I work on acceptance. The Serenity Prayer comes in extremely handy here. Having the serenity to accept the things I cannot change and the courage to change the things

I can is very important. Having the wisdom to know the difference is, by far, my most important asset. Still, there are situations that seem to blur the lines. Here is an example.

I drank and drugged for many, many years—twenty-five years, give or take a couple. Again, I was able to quit drugs, but I had a difficult time finding true recovery and getting my life back because I had a problem quitting drinking. Drugs were part of my past, and I would be dishonest if I did not acknowledge the role they played in my life. Yet they played a lesser role compared to my drinking. Still, I was not born with all the answers, and it took time for me to find recovery and to break the hold alcohol had on my life. I have to remind myself that all things take time. My life took many twists and turns to get me where I am today, but I had to start somewhere.

I regretted the fact that I had "wasted" so much of my life. It was, by far, my greatest regret. It is still the biggest regret I can think of since becoming sober. For quite some time I thought there was nothing that I could do about my past drinking and drugging to alleviate this regret. Since I could think of nothing else to do, I prayed. It is funny the way I sometimes expend all my options before I pray. The answer came to me: There was and still is something I could do, and I do it to the best of my ability. I use my drinking as an example to help young people not repeat my mistake. (This is in line with the idea of making "living amends" in Step Nine.) It does not give me those years back, but it does help to ease my regret and it keeps me in touch with people who are newer in recovery. It helps my recovery "stay young." In the process, I help other people—especially young people—to enter recovery and find happiness. Instead of feeling guilt over something in my past, I have found a way to turn it into something good. In the process,

I have forgiven myself for drinking for such a large part of my life. The guilt has weakened to the point where I no longer have a desire to kick myself because of my drinking. If the desire to kick myself appears, I remind myself that I no longer drink and that I am doing what I can to turn it into something good. Then I remind myself that I have forgiven myself for my past offenses.

Guilt over past drinking and worry about future drinking robs me of my recovery today. I have no more reasons to feel guilty about my past drinking. It is over and done with, and I need to let it remain in the past. As for worrying about future drinking: I tend to believe this worry is based on my guilt over past drinking. I have no other real basis for this worry. I have been in recovery for some time now. Why do I have to worry I may pick up again? I offer the guilt I may hold over past drinking as the culprit, and I make this offer with good reason. Since I forgave myself for my past drinking and found a way to put it to good use by helping others, I find that I do not worry about drinking in the future. Instead, I continue to do the things I need to do to remain in recovery: prayer and meditation, step work, meeting attendance, working with a sponsor and others, and service.

Like everything else in life, there is a process to picking up. I must think about it for a good length of time, then I must act on the thought. I must go to the store, make my purchase, and then consume it. Today, I have no reason to follow this process to its logical conclusion. I know the results—I will lose. Why would I go down that road? Why would I ruin what I have by picking up? The answer is that I would not. The truth is, unless I take a drink, I will not get drunk. There is little chance that I will walk down the street, be held at gunpoint, and be forced to drink alcohol.

The chance that I will accidentally consume alcohol is equally remote if I take a few simple precautions. It is the guilt over past drinking that causes me to worry about the possibility of future episodes. There can be no other answer for me today.

Guilt is a form of condemnation, and condemnation used to be a great reason to drink. Once I condemned myself, once my own disapproval of who I was became strong enough—which did not take much effort in my heavy drinking days—a drink seemed the next proper move. Removing the guilt in my life—especially my guilt over drinking—has freed me to stop worrying about the potential of future drinking. All I really have to do is stay sober right now. The future will take care of itself. Unless there is more I can do—like helping others—to relieve my guilt over past drinking, I must accept that forgiveness is enough, and, although forgiveness can be enough, I have found that helping others find recovery is the absolute best path to finding true forgiveness in this area of my life.

I need to learn to love myself for who I am, for who I have become, and for who I will be in the future. Guilt is a roadblock separating me from love. If I claim I am a bad person and if I allow myself to feel guilty because I drank too much—or for any other reason, for that matter—I delay my potential for self-love. The longer I delay loving myself, the more potential I have for finding fault and feeling guilty. Setting guilt aside through forgiveness and helping others allows me to find ways to love who I am today. I must do whatever is necessary to rid myself of guilt in order to love myself today, because the guilt I hold against myself is there due to my past behavior.

In order to love who I am today, I must accept my past, because it has made me who I am. If it were not for my past, there would be no me in the here and now. I am exactly who and where I am today because of who I used to be and what I have done. If I condemn my past, I condemn my present. If I condemn my present, my future is also condemned, and by my own choice.

I MUST CONSCIOUSLY DECIDE

TO DO THINGS OF WHICH

I AM AFRAID. I MUST DO THIS

ON A CONSISTENT BASIS.

SUCCESS OR FAILURE MUST

NOT BE TOO LARGE A PART OF

THE EQUATION, BECAUSE IF

I ATTEMPT TO DO SOMETHING

THAT I AM AFRAID OF,

I SUCCEED.

8

THE FEAR FACTOR

Fear is also a roadblock to getting rid of guilt. Fear plays a larger part in ridding myself of guilt than I like to admit. I found that when I looked deep enough, I was afraid to get rid of my guilt. I thought I was supposed to feel guilty about my past drinking. I have found this to be a big lie because no one expects me to feel guilty except me, and this is one expectation I need to lose. Another fear I held was that if I did not feel guilty, other people might think I was crazy, or that I was maybe a little pompous. Today, I do not care so much about what other people think about me. This comes from letting go of guilt as well. Since fear plays such a big part in holding me back and keeping me from becoming the person I would like to be, it is worth a deeper look.

Overcoming fear does not mean what I used to think it meant. I used to believe overcoming fear meant that I was supposed to be fearless, and that I was supposed to be able not to feel afraid. This is just plain wrong. Saying "don't be afraid" is misguided aid. It cannot be done. I have found that I cannot simply make fear go away by thinking or wishing it would leave me alone. To get rid of fear I must learn to walk through it, and I must do this repeatedly. I learned this by doing it. My first sponsor repeatedly pushed me through what I have come to call "walls of fear." He did so until I concluded that fear is overcome not through sheer willpower, but through courageous action.

Courageous action is also something I had to redefine, because my definition of courage used to be, quite simply, the absence of fear. I thought in order to have courage I had to rid myself of any fear whatsoever. My experiences have led me to a new understanding of what courage is and what it is not. Courage is not the absence of fear. Courageous people are afraid too. Courage means my taking proper action even though I am afraid. It is walking through the wall of fear.

My first sponsor pushed me through wall after wall of fear. He did not do this literally; he did not really even push me in a figurative sense. He gave me suggestions and things to do that helped me to realize just how fragile fear can be. When I took the first suggestion I had no idea of what I was getting into, which is probably a good thing, because I might have shied away from the task. I might have even run away screaming if I had known what was coming. This is because while fear is fragile, it is also powerful in appearance. Fear looks like a big monster. Until I discovered fear could not hurt me without my permission, I refused to approach it with anything more than jest-filled intention. Until I learned through experience that I could walk through fear and survive, I refused to approach it with any seriousness. If I was afraid of something, I avoided it and instead moved on to something I found to be less frightening.

While fear was difficult to overcome on the first few occasions, I have reduced the impact it has in my life today, and I do my best to walk through fear whenever and wherever necessary. I especially follow this mode of operation if I believe fear may be holding back my spiritual growth. The biggest wall of fear I walked through, because it was the first real wall I hit, was extremely frightening; every fear-wall since has been smaller, thanks to this experience. Although I may have thought fear was going to kill me, I soon discovered it did not have that kind of power.

My sponsor told me to memorize "How It Works," which is read at the beginning of most meetings. It is about two and a half pages long, and it took me some time to memorize, but I did as he asked. After I told him I had it down and he checked me on it, I picked him up for our usual Friday meeting. This meeting is a little different from many others I have attended because they do not read "How It Works" at the beginning. Everyone usually gives their recovery date when they share. I had counted the years of recovery prior to this day and knew there would be in the neighborhood of 650 years of recovery in the room—on average, fifteen to twenty years per person. I had been sober for about four months when this took place. I was afraid, to say the least, because I knew my sponsor's intention was to have me recite "How It Works" for this crowd. I did my best to "not be afraid," but that was not working. I was a nervous wreck. I had no business telling these people how it works—I was there to learn from them. Little did I know what I was to learn that day.

My sponsor, who often led this group, started the meeting a couple minutes early by saying, "Today we are going to hear 'How It Works,' because my pigeon here (he enjoyed calling me his pigeon; I enjoyed the old-fashioned term as well) is going to recite it for us. Go ahead now; let's see how far you can get." The room was deathly silent; I could hear my heartbeat in my ears. I could feel my pulse in my head. My hands were shaking; I sat on them to keep them from giving me away. I felt small beads of sweat pop up on my scalp and decided, since there was no way out, that I had better begin and do my best to forget about showing my fear—as I knew I would. I glanced around the room and noticed every one of the twenty-five or thirty people there was looking straight at me. I swallowed—it felt like cotton balls—and cleared my throat.

I began reciting slowly. The first sentence gone, I took in some air and noticed breathing was difficult. My legs were shaking. But I continued because I wanted more than anything to have what my sponsor had, and somehow I knew this was part of my getting there. I could not breathe; I felt like my end was near at hand. Halfway through, I started to relax—comparatively speaking. I began taking air better, but it was hard to talk because my mouth was dry. My tongue stuck to the roof of my mouth like a spider web to a broom. My vision darkened around the edges. I paused for more air, only slightly, though, because I did not want anyone to think I was unsure of what came next, and I was not, even though I thought I might be dying. I never stumbled over a word. I did not hesitate, and finally I finished to a smattering of applause. There were a few people who, for whatever reason, clapped their hands. I told them, "Please don't do that, I only did this because he made me," pointing to my sponsor. Little did I know, at that moment, how much I had done it for myself.

It took me nearly the entire hour-long meeting to get my composure back. Even though I thought I might die, I did not. I felt fear like I had never felt it before, and it did not kill me. I had learned a lesson as necessary as breathing, and it helped me become who I am today. My feelings will not kill me. No matter how good or bad I think they might be at that moment, my feelings are just passing through, and I should learn to enjoy them. I have even learned to enjoy feeling sad. I have learned to let sadness go when it is time. Today, I do my best to feel my feelings, to enjoy even the most difficult ones to the best of my ability, and then let them go when the time comes. I learned this by experiencing fear like I had never felt it before, by feeling fear I actually thought might kill me and surviving to tell the tale.

What would have happened if I had not made it all the way through? How would I have reacted? I will honestly admit I have no idea what the short-term effects might have been, but I can tell you that my sponsor told me what would have happened in the long term, because I asked him on the way home from the meeting. After I told him I thought I was a goner a couple of times, that I did not know if I would survive the discomfort, the dry mouth, the shaking, and the sweats, I asked him what would have happened if I had not made it all the way through. He answered in a quite matter-of-fact tone, "There's always next week."

"I thought I was happy before that I got it right; now I couldn't be happier to have made it all the way through. That was the most horrendous thing I have ever done, and I'm glad it's over."

"There's always next week," he replied.

I went numb. "Are you going to make me do that again? Next week?"

"I didn't make you do it today."

"Sure you did. You were behind the whole thing. You made me memorize it, you checked me on it, then you made me recite it before all those people."

"Hey," he calmly claimed, "don't blame me for the things you do. I only make suggestions. If you choose to follow those suggestions, that is your choice. I can't make you do anything."

"Well, I'm not blaming you," I stuttered. "I was just saying, this all happened because of you."

"But it didn't happen because of me," he replied. "It happened because of you. I made suggestions. You took action. You did the work, the memorization; you did the recitation. All I did was provide an opportunity. You took the opportunity and used it for your personal growth. You do the work, you take the action, and you live with the consequences—good or bad. Remember, not all consequences are bad. I know this may sound old, but if I had suggested you jump off a cliff, would you have done it?"

"No."

"Then, you see, the final choice is yours, and you generally make those choices based upon what you think the consequences will be. You should not give me blame or credit for your choices and actions. You must be willing to accept both for yourself." Then he added, "Next week we will do it again."

"Really?" I asked, and although I had decided I would simply do what he suggested because I trusted him and knew he wanted to help me become the best person I could be, I asked, "Why?"

"You will see."

The next week, I did it again, and I did see. It was ever-so-much easier than the week before. Nevertheless, I was still full of fear. Even though I had been practicing all week to make sure I had it down solid, I was very nervous. Yet I could breathe better, I did not sweat as much, and my mouth did not fill with desert sand! Most importantly, I *knew* I would not die. I had walked through the same fear again, and although it was still a huge fear the second time through, the impact was vastly diminished. Fear was losing its grip on me in this area of my life.

I actually got to the point where I would recite "How It Works" at many meetings. I did this for several months, actually. I would hold the card as I recited, but I would look around the room, not at the paper. Quite often, people would come up to me later to ask if I had memorized "How It Works," if I were reciting it from memory. I would tell them I had indeed memorized it, and that it was part of my overcoming fear in my life. If they wanted to talk about it, we would. In the process, I was overcoming another fear, although I did not realize it at the time.

I was losing my fear of what other people thought of me. I had to, because I am sure there were people who did not come up to me to ask about my recital, and instead chose to decide what they thought without my input. I was becoming okay with that, even though I was sure they thought I was showing off. I was gradually becoming accustomed to my fear. I knew that it could not kill me.

There is one important footnote to this story. A recitation of "How It Works" took place at many meetings where there was no printed card or book available. The chairperson said it looked like we would have to forgo the reading of "How It Works," because we had nothing from which to read. Another person, having seen me recite it before, said I knew it by heart, and that I didn't need to read it. The chairperson asked me if I would "read" it for the group. I began without a nervous thought; fear had no time to find me. However, about halfway through I got lost, and fell silent while trying to find my place. Someone prompted me, and off I went again, only to find myself lost again, and in need of another prompt. I do not remember how many times I was prompted during that "reading," but I do remember it was rather embarrassing to have someone else tell the group I knew it by heart only to have me fail to recite it smoothly.

I sat through the meeting feeling humbled and disappointed with my failure. After the meeting, a couple of people came up to me to thank me for my contribution. I stumbled through a thank you, making sure to mention my errors. This happened before I learned to say "thank you" and then to shut up. In each case, they waved off the missteps with nonchalance, thanking me again because, as they said, the reading of "How It Works" is a very important part of the meeting experience for them—even if there are errors. One of these people even told me he thought he could recite it, just not in front of a crowd as I did. We had a talk about how I came to be relatively comfortable doing just that and why I had gone through the agony of the first attempt. Before he left, he said he planned to talk to his sponsor about attempting the exercise. To this day, I have no idea if he followed through on his promise. I do know this experience helped me learn about failure and my fear of failing.

As I said, this kind of thing happened more than once. When there was nothing to read from, I would recite. In fact, I have attended meetings where there was nothing to read from and someone else did the reciting, which I consider a wonderful thing—for them and for me. While I was inwardly cheering them on, I was humbled to discover other people could not only do what I had done, but were willing to put themselves on the line. Some of them made it all the way through, and just like me they sometimes needed a prompt or two, which I was not too quick to give, for I wanted them to have a chance to continue unaided. More often than not, I would give them more time than others deemed necessary, and they would receive a cue from someone else. I began to see just how common it is for people to know "How It Works" well enough to recite it if they want to. I have learned to encourage people to give it a try if they are so inclined. If they are willing to try, they usually succeed, although they may need a cue or two along the way.

My loss of fear about reciting "How It Works" has translated into a loss of fear in many other areas of my life because I have found fear to be more of an alarm or warning than a life-threatening condition. Because of this loss of fear, I have learned to push myself through many more walls of fear—especially the wall surrounding failure.

I have found fear of success to be a form of fearing failure. My fear of success stems from the idea that if I "get it right" once, people will expect me to be able to repeat whatever it is I have succeeded at accomplishing. This is another example of erroneous thinking, for many reasons. One reason is that most people realize we are human; we all make mistakes, even while performing tasks with which we are familiar. I have come to understand this myself, and have even come up with an example I like to remind myself of when I have made a mistake or failed at something, even something I had become relatively familiar with or something I should have been able to do without much trouble.

I think of baseball players. They practice hitting the ball. They get so good at hitting the ball that they become professionals and are paid millions of dollars a year to play the game. They practice, practice, and practice some more. It is, after all, their job. Yet, despite all this practice, despite the fact that it is their job to hit the ball, they often do not—they often miss, or somehow make an out. They fail in their job. What then do we say as fans? "Can't hit 'em all, right?" That's what we say. We accept the fact that a professional baseball player, whose job it is to practice hitting and then apply it in a game situation, gets a hit at best only about one in three times at bat. Of course, baseball would not be much of a game if they could hit them all. Getting a hit one-third of the time is still thought of as being above average. Batting .400 (getting a hit 40 percent of the time) is outstanding, record-making ball play.

Baseball players fail more than they succeed—that is, they don't hit more often than they do hit—yet the fans, owners, and sportswriters think nothing of this fact. Why then should I be overly concerned about getting everything right all the time—especially when I do not practice it every day? Even if I do practice something every day, I should cut myself a little slack. Fearing failure is really my fearing the inevitable, and fearing success is generally fearing the ensuing failures or mistakes, which are also inevitable.

Mostly, my fear of failure boils down to the second reason I hold this fear, which is simply that I fear what other people think about me. I am worried people will think bad things about me if I fail or make a mistake. This is the most bizarre thing, yet I used to let it run my life. I used to believe everyone was sitting around and waiting for me to fail, so they could think bad things about me. How self-centered is this? First, most people do not care whether I succeed or fail; this includes my acquaintances. Most people are too busy with their own lives to give a hoot about what I do. Second, and probably most importantly, the people who do care about me certainly do not sit around waiting for me to fail so they can talk trash about me. They are there when I do fail to help me put things right again.

The truth is that I have found it a good barometer of our relationship to tell those who really care about me about my failures. This is not to say I fail intentionally in order to see who will come to my aid, but I do know the people who do come to my aid when I fail are my real friends. The folks who want to talk poorly about me because of my failings are not my friends. They are, in fact, gossiping. Don't we already know what gossip is? So let them talk if they must; it is nothing but gossip, and they really are not talking about me anyway. They are talking about themselves; they are only using my name as camouflage.

Dealing with fear is something we must do. It is something we actually have instincts for, but I believe these instincts are outdated. The fight-or-flight instinct tells us that when there is a threat, we have two options: We can stay and fight or run away. These instincts worked well before we became civilized and fighting became socially and legally unacceptable. Except for wars, we no longer really have the option to fight without the possibility of going to jail.

Today, the fight seems more a mental thing for me, a form of metaphor for standing up to the actual fear. Flight still means relatively the same thing: I run away—literally or figuratively—from a fearful situation; I do not deal with a problem or issue. In society today, the fight-or-flight process takes place mostly in my head. What used to be instinct—something that took place in a heartbeat—I now have to stop to think about. It is uncomfortable. Fear causes fight or flight and is always uncomfortable.

When fear comes along, I must make a decision—to fight or fly—and then I must follow through on my decision. Since I cannot actually fight, I must carry the fear with me until I have taken action or until the issue is resolved. Sometimes flight can cause as much fear as the fighting, or even more. Running from my fear can cause me more tension and stress than actually standing up to the fear and doing what I know to be the right thing, although quite often running can seem like the softer, easier way. I have to choose wisely, which is a learned process, a process of trial and error, a process of success and failure. I will make mistakes when dealing with fear, just as I will make mistakes in life in general. It is important for me to remember mistakes are not the end of anything—failure is a learning opportunity.

Fear is limiting. It holds me back from doing things I would really like to do. I cannot count the times in my life when fear has kept me from doing, or at least trying for, something I truly desired. Most of my regrets in life are concerned with things I have left undone due to fear. Quite often, I did not even realize it was fear holding me back; however, as I look over my past, I see quite clearly how fear has affected my life. I have found it has almost never really been an ally. Sure, it has kept me out of a few scrapes where I could have been physically hurt, but the majority of the time, fear has simply kept me from attaining goals I would like to have reached.

Today, however, I am going after some of the things I have left undone because I have discovered the truth about fear: Fear has limits. Since the day I recited "How It Works" to a group of people who had been sober many years longer than I had and found that fear could not kill me, I have taken a good look at how I have let fear affect me over the years. I found almost none of its effect has been to my advantage. I decided to see what I could do to overcome fear, because it seems to do no more than hold me back. What I have discovered is that there are only so many fears—so many things to be afraid of—and all fear boils down to a few things. My fear can usually fit into two categories: The first is of not getting something I desire; the second is of losing something I wish to keep.

I can call it fear of failure, which is really fear of what other people will think of me if I fail, but the truth is, my fear is based on losing my good standing in the eyes of others. The funniest thing about this fear is that I may not have this good standing to begin with—it may be an illusion or a delusion I am carrying with regard to how others think about me. After all, if people really cared about me and wanted me to succeed, they certainly would not think I was a bad person because I failed. They might feel bad for me, they might want to help, but they would not bad-mouth me and they would not think less of me as a person because I tried and did not succeed. The people who will talk poorly of me because I fail are people who do not really care for me to begin with. I have decided that the people who are willing to think less of me because I tried and failed do not have my best interests in mind. While I am willing to let them have their fun at my expense, I no longer give their comments much credit. After all, they probably have not tried to do the very thing I just attempted and failed at. Maybe they never will, because they themselves are full of fear. Talking poorly about me, as well as my failures, may be the only way they have to feel better about not making the attempt on their own. This attitude has helped me deal with fear in a way that is beneficial to my personal growth.

I am learning to let people be who they are, do what they do, and say what they say. All the while, I have decided to be myself. I will do what I do and say what I say. Most importantly, I will do what I say I will do. To the best of my ability, I will do the things I say I will do because keeping my commitments improves my self-esteem, and I have found a strong self-esteem to be a great advantage when it comes to overcoming fear. Still, the greatest way to overcome fear for me is to face it repeatedly.

I must consciously decide to do things of which I am afraid. I must do this on a consistent basis. Success or failure must not be too large a part of the equation, because if I attempt to do something that I am afraid of, I succeed. Even if I do not attain the results I desire, the attempt is a success because I faced my fear. Truth is, the outcome is often not my decision anyway. It is only up to me to make the attempt, do my best, then let God take care of the results. If the outcome is not to my liking, I can try again. I must remember—failure is a teacher. Failure is a beginning. Failure is not the end.

One of the easiest ways I have found to face fear is to take a good, hard look at that of which I am *really* afraid. You may be thinking that sounds simple, but it really is more complicated than that, because fear is an insidious force. Fear wants me to think I am afraid of something large, something I cannot overcome. The truth is that fear is smaller than it appears. Fear somehow has the ability to appear much larger than it really is.

I had a friend who was thinking of moving to South Carolina. Most of her family lived there, and she wanted to be closer to them. However, she was afraid to make the move. She began telling me about her fears. She is legally blind, and for her, just getting around can be a challenge. She was used to her current surroundings and was afraid that she might not be able to find a living situation where transportation would be as accessible as it was where she lived. She had a good job and was afraid she might not be able to find one to replace it. She was afraid of the actual move, and how she would go about getting everything packed and transported. Her list went on, and if you use your imagination just a little, I am sure you can come up with a few fears you might have around moving five states away.

I suggested she write her fears down on a piece of paper. I had never done this myself; in fact, the idea had never occurred to me, but it sounded like a good idea. I felt certain the idea had come from God, since it came from nowhere within me, I was sure, and I had never tried it myself, but it sounded sensible. I told her I had never tried this myself, but that I thought it might just help her to see her fear for what it really was. She took this advice and wrote down all the things she was afraid of about the possible move. Six months later, she was living in South Carolina.

A few months after she successfully faced her fear and moved, I had the opportunity to put this method of facing fears to good use. A wonderful opportunity to organize a hotline in my town emerged, yet I became paralyzed by fear. I had run my mouth about how we should provide a twenty-four-hour hotline manned by volunteers who were in recovery instead of paying a professional answering service, which had no experience, strength, or hope to offer. I suddenly had the job of making it happen. My first thought was that I had opened my mouth and inserted my foot. Then, when the fear set in ferociously and I wanted to back out, I remembered the suggestion I had given my friend regarding her fear about moving. I made a list of my fears. I was afraid people would not sign up to do the work, or that the whole thing would be a flop; I would fail miserably or people would sign up, then not show up to work their shift. I would not have enough bright ideas to get the thing going, and I would not get the help I needed. I wrote down these fears and more. Then I took a good look at them. They really boiled down to two things—fear of what other people might think of me (especially if I failed), and fear of not being in control. If I failed, I feared people would talk poorly about me. Since I could not control the situation—it was outside of my own actions—I had fears about all the things I could not control.

Seeing my fears for what they were, I did what I could do. For the most part that consisted of making a schedule, printing some fliers, and asking for help getting the word out that we needed volunteers. Then I started working phone shifts—pretty much all the shifts that were not covered with volunteers. Oh, and I prayed.

Well, things worked out. We now have our phones manned twenty-four hours a day by people in recovery. I was able to face the fear by writing it down and taking a good look at what it was that I really feared. When I did that, the fears looked pretty silly, to be honest, and as I look back on my part in the whole thing I see that what I did was one person's part. I did what I could. The key to success was that eighty-plus other people did what they could, too; they continue to do what they can to make the hotline the success it is today. I left my role as chairperson some time ago, and others have taken over the chairperson's spot. They have since added new ideas, which have made things even better. However, the volunteers make the whole thing happen. They do the real work.

Probably the greatest lesson I learned from the entire experience is the value of writing down my fears. Once I wrote them down, I could see them for their silliness. I continue this practice today, and I plan to do so for the rest of my days. When I find fears holding me back, I write them down. Then I look at them until I see them for what they really are. Once I see the truth, my fear begins to dissolve and I am able to summon the courage to do my part—and I am willing to let other people do their part as well.

Today I see fear for what it is: an overinflated bully who needs only a good look to be seen through. When I take the time to see through my fears—to see them for what they really are—I find it is not too hard to summon the courage necessary to walk through the wall they represent. The more times I do the exercise, the easier it gets to repeat the process. As I practice overcoming fear, I become better at accomplishing the task and my fear diminishes. When I stop feeding fear, it begins to die. While fear will probably never die completely, it does weaken as I feed my courage and become ever stronger.

I USED TO SAY, "I HAVE

A PROBLEM WITH THAT,"

ALL THE TIME. IT ROLLED

OFF MY TONGUE LIKE WATER

FLOWING DOWNSTREAM.

ONE DAY, IT OCCURRED TO ME

THAT IF I STOPPED TALKING

AFTER THE FOURTH WORD,

I WOULD REACH THE

BEGINNING OF A SOLUTION.

"I HAVE A PROBLEM."

9

RESENTMENT

Resentment is a big, greedy fish in a small pond. At one time, it not only ate what I gave it; it tried to devour me as well, even though (or perhaps because) I fed it. Resentment seems to bite the hand that feeds it. The more I learn about resentment, the more I find it to be something I want to avoid. I see finding relief from resentments to be a big part of becoming normal. It seems that many people have difficulty with resentments, both in and out of recovery. I discovered that in this regard I was as normal as anyone else; yet for someone in recovery, resentments are an unaffordable luxury. I had to learn to quit feeding my resentments.

I discovered I was spiritually sick, and when I looked at why I was angry, I found it was because of fear. Usually I was angry because my self-esteem, my pocketbook, my ambitions, or my relationships were, in some way, threatened. In short, I was sore about something, but at the time, I was unsure of exactly what it was. I was usually unable to forgive the person I saw as the threat.

In dealing with resentments, I've found that forgiveness is the key. In the beginning, I despised the idea of forgiving people who had hurt me. As I learned more about forgiveness, I discovered I was forgiving them not for their sake, but for my own. After all, they do not receive peace of mind from my forgiveness. I do.

Almost everyone has heard that holding onto resentments is like drinking poison while hoping one's "enemy" dies as a result. This is so true that it loses its capacity for comedy, although I do laugh at the idea because on the surface it sounds kind of funny. However, when I look at it in depth, any potential for humor is soon washed away. I used to do this very thing. I used to get drunk *at* people. Someone would hurt me; while the hurt might be real or imagined, I would show them by getting drunk, literally by taking poison. Alcohol is a toxic substance. The word intoxicant, which is what alcohol is, has the word toxic as its root. For me, especially, alcohol is poison. It really has only one purpose for an addict, and that is to kill—while making life miserable in the process. When I was using in order to get rid of resentment, or when I was using to "get back at someone," I was, quite literally, taking poison and hoping the other person would die, or at least suffer, as a result. While this is obviously flawed thinking, the sad thing is that it made perfect sense at the time. Fortunately, I have learned better. Today, I know the key to living a resentment-free life.

Learning how to forgive is relatively easy. Putting it into practice is another issue altogether. How to forgive—the best way I have found—comes from a story about how effective and powerful forgiveness can be. I forgive everyone who has ever harmed me. Some of my resentments went so deep that I had to pray for more than two weeks, while some took more than a month; however, eventually I found I was free from resentment in every case. Not only was I free from resentment, but I found I actually felt love for the person I resented. I can honestly say I love my ex-wife more today than I ever did while we were married, even though she still will have nothing to do with me. That is her resentment, and she can keep it as long as she wishes. It does not affect me or the way I feel toward her today.

While praying for the other person is a wonderful way to forgive, especially those hard cases, I've found that many of my resentments can be avoided altogether if I am willing to forgive instantly. I still enjoy a little instant gratification and instant forgiveness can provide it, because it makes me feel better in a flash. The question is, "How do I learn to instantly forgive someone?" The solution was so simple it eluded me. However, I finally found it hiding right under my nose. Of course, the main reason I did not recognize the answer is because it runs contrary to my all-too-common line of thought, the line of thought I am still working to change.

What I found is simple, and so easy to do that it is almost scary. I discovered a way to forgiveness like no other I had ever encountered. While I am sure many people have used this way for years, if not centuries, at the time it was brand-new to me.

It boils down to "giving the benefit of the doubt that I would like to have given to me."

The simplest way I know to go about giving the benefit of the doubt to others is to make up excuses for them. I am a pro at making up excuses—I have had years of practice—and while I do my best not to use (or need) excuses for myself these days, I have put this skill to use on behalf of people who offend me in some way.

I do not like using or needing excuses because I find them to be unnecessary. I believe society has shown me that I must explain my mistakes, misdeeds, and errors, but I have the experience to show my excuses are really only for me. They do not necessarily appease the person receiving them; they only calm my own mind. As I mentioned earlier, when I am late picking up a friend, my tendency is to give an excuse for my tardiness. However, my excuse does little to relieve them of the worry they suffered or the time they wasted waiting for me. My excuse only calms my mind. It does this because I am okay with the excuse given. When I combine this excuse with forgiveness—done for my peace of mind—the math is simple.

Since forgiveness is for my own benefit, and excuses only benefit me, it makes perfect sense to make excuses for people when they provide me with cause for a grievance. I make an excuse for them. I accept the excuse as plausible (after all, I made it up); then I can forgive the offense.

I began experimenting with this theory while driving, and it worked like a charm from the very start. I was driving along, minding my own business, obeying the traffic laws, when from out of nowhere—well actually, from the right-hand side of the road—a guy pulled out right in front of me. In this case, I had to hit the brakes rather hard to avoid a collision; however, it does not take a large inconvenience for the tactic to work. This person, whom I did not know, had caused me a rather large discomfort. I had to hit the brakes and I was afraid—if only for a fraction of an instant—otherwise, I might have hit him. I went through all the stages of discontent that arise from a near-accident such as this.

My first instinct was to cuss, swear, and show him how mad I was. Fortunately, I was able to hold off—again using procrastination—just long enough to remember my new experiment, and I went to work making up an excuse for his actions. The excuse came to me as easily as sliding down a greased pole, and it was a good one, too. I rationalized that he was on his way to the hospital, his wife had been ill, and he got the call that she was going to die. He was on his way to see his wife for the last time. While I knew in the back of my mind the odds of this being true were outlandish, I found it impossible to be angry with him because if it were true—if he really was on his way to see his wife for the last time—there was every reason for him to pull out in front of me. He would be in a hurry and he would be distracted, to name just two possible things. I gave him the benefit of the doubt—probably more than was necessary, for I am a pro at excuses—and it relieved my stress, my anger, and any potential for resentment.

I have done this for long enough so that the only excuse I give other drivers is: "They are doing the best they can." While their best might not be good enough to suit me, the excuse implies they can do no better at this moment. Therefore, I must accept their current level of competence. I am a much calmer driver thanks to "giving the benefit of the doubt" to others, since nearly every venture into public for me begins with driving and dealing with other drivers.

Being able to arrive at my destination in a calm mood is my favor to myself and to those I will deal with when I arrive at my destination. The nice thing about this particular excuse is its universality. I can use they are doing the best they can in any situation, for any person. I seem to be able to accept that people are doing their best, even when their best seems inadequate. Because of this new attitude, I can apply the Serenity Prayer to all areas of my life. If I can change something, I do. If I cannot change the situation, I conclude that my acceptance of the situation is enough of a response.

This method of acceptance works nearly every time I employ it. The times it does not seem to work are times when "I know too much" to make a good excuse. These cases generally involve people I am very familiar with, such as family and friends, and I seem to think they should know better. Under these circumstances, it can be very difficult to forgive instantly. Still, if I find myself heading toward a resentment I know I will need to forgive at some point—for my own good—it is best to get an early start. If I can remember they are doing the best they can—they are probably upset too, and nobody does their best work when they are upset—it becomes much easier to begin to forgive. It is my job to forgive, for it is my problem if I do not.

I used to say, "I have a problem with that," all the time. It rolled off my tongue like water flowing downstream. One day, it occurred to me that if I stopped talking after the fourth word, I would reach the beginning of a solution. "I have a problem." It really does not matter if the problem is with you, this, that, or the other thing. The problem is mine, and when I take ownership of it, I can begin to do something about it. As long as I leave ownership of the problem with you, this, that, or the other thing, I give up control over how I feel with regard to the situation. If I have a problem I can do nothing about, now that's a problem.

The first and most difficult step in solving a problem, though I do not like to admit it, is to take ownership. It is my problem. The next, and easier, step is the definition. I must identify my problem. If I can rustle up the honesty to take ownership of the problem, discovery of the actual issue is usually pretty easy. All I have to do is remain honest in order to see my part in the conflict. Having the problem defined usually leads to a solution. While this is not always the case, I was surprised to find just how much truth is contained in the saying, "A problem well defined is half-solved." If I have been honest enough to get this far, it should be easy enough to hold onto honesty just long enough to see that the solution usually lies within me.

I must take action, or, in other words, I must change. Since change is inevitable and constant, why do I get so worked up about it? Growth requires change, and problems are opportunities for growth. When I began to see the truth of this fact—that problems are opportunities— my attitude changed and my paradigm shifted. Once my paradigm shifted and I began to see opportunities where I once saw problems, it became much easier for me to take ownership of the problems. After all, I do not mind owning an opportunity.

This paradigm shift did not happen overnight, and it did not take place without some help. Again, my first sponsor was at the root of the alteration to my thinking process. I called him one night with a problem. After our traditional greeting, I said:

"I have a problem—"

"Opportunity," he interrupted.

"No," I went on, "I have a problem—"

"Opportunity," he interrupted again.

Frustrated, first by the problem and now by his insistence that it *wasn't* a problem—even without hearing any details—I said, "No, you don't understand. This is a real problem. Don't you want to hear what it is?"

"There are no problems, there are only opportunities," he calmly stated.

I fell silent, while pondering the possibility that he might be right. Could it be true? If so, how could it be possible? What would it be like to live a life without problems? Slowly, it began to sink in that what I had on my hands was not really a problem after all. It *was* an opportunity. This came to me because I could see the opportunity within the problem. I believed that every cloud had a silver lining, so I began to wonder if every problem contained an opportunity. I still needed help with my current "opportunity," and I needed more time to think about this crazy idea I had just been given. I said, "All right, I have an opportunity." Then I went on to explain my situation.

We discussed my issue at length. After a while, I could not help but see it as an opportunity, and not really a problem at all. Sure, it was a difficult issue; most things I consider problems are, but I was seeing this one in an entirely new light. It somehow lost much of its weight. I began to take ownership of the opportunity. Soon I began to see what the real issues were. The real issues were mine, not the other person's. The other person was doing the best he could at the time. I was probably doing the best I could at the time as well. Our best was just not good enough to resolve the issues at hand. I walked away with a problem and resentment.

Fortunately, I managed to turn this problem into an opportunity, and it has helped me to do the same with other problems. In fact, today I do my best to see all my problems as opportunities. I find it easier to take ownership of an opportunity than I do a problem. Also, when I see problems as opportunities, I am not as inclined to wait for someone else to do something about them. I do not lay blame on someone else. I do not tend to believe it is their problem. I do not think, "I am right and they are wrong." I simply see potential. Potential leads me to solutions, resolutions, and possibilities for growth.

Since my problems are mine, I must take responsibility for them. Seeing them as opportunities and seeing potential for change as a good thing may not come easily at first. However, with some practice, it can become almost second nature.

I used to run from problems because it takes work to change. Changing old habits can be difficult and uncomfortable. Fear likes to stick its ugly head in and tell me I am better off not changing. Fear lies to me. Where I have problems, I have resentments, and resentments are dangerous to my health and well-being. Not only are resentments dangerous, but having them is much more uncomfortable than not having them. The key is to get some momentum going and move toward change.

In order to gain momentum toward anything, I have to first stop moving away from it. I must stop running away from my problems and my resentments in order to begin moving toward my opportunities. Of course, to do this I will be face-to-face with my fear. Facing fear will be easier if I understand that what I am trying to do will benefit me greatly. In this case, it will definitely be highly beneficial. Shifting my paradigm from seeing problems to seeing opportunities has changed my life in the direction of the positive in a manner that I cannot adequately explain. Suffice it to say, the payoff has been worth far more than I have invested. The actual work I have done seems minuscule when viewed alongside the tremendous gains I have made.

The shortest distance from resentment to forgiveness is a straight line—through the issue, seeing the opportunity—without the usual side trips of laying blame, pointing fingers, or justifying the ways in which I am right and they are wrong. The quickest way to serenity and relief from resentment is to own my part and to forgive the other person their faults, for I know that I have enough of my own.

Freedom from resentment comes from being comfortable enough with myself to allow others to be themselves. The only way I know to become comfortable with who I am is to make the changes I find necessary. They will present themselves as opportunities, and they will do so willingly and without a fight. I must learn to see myself as an ever-changing person while learning to ask myself if I want to become better or if I am willing to settle for less. I have found that settling for less is unacceptable because it means that eventually I will suffer.

I made the biggest change in my life when I quit using. I had put it off for so long that the suffering was unbearable. In the beginning, the change was excruciatingly difficult because I was very deeply entrenched in my ways. When I finally did quit, I proved to myself just how capable I am of changing. Now only one question remains: Am I willing to become more flexible, more accepting of change, or will I continue to fight and struggle and suffer through the upcoming inevitable changes, the same way I suffered through my addiction and the quitting therefrom? Taking change in small doses seems to be the easiest way. When it comes to getting rid of resentment, I have found a powerful way to change my attitude. Resentments are problems; problems are opportunities. I like to take advantage of opportunities because opportunities help me grow.

Resentment can be defined as indignation or ill will felt as a result of a real or imagined offense.

This definition shows just how silly resentments are. Indignation isn't any fun. Ill will is no fun, either. While I could often say I allow myself to feel resentful because the offense is real, I find my imagination is rather strong as well. Regardless of whether the offenses are real or imagined, the indignation and ill will are always real—and they are always a choice. When I choose resentment, I choose to feel the indignation and ill will. I do this instead of choosing to be happy, joyous, and free. Now that's crazy.

My first sponsor liked to say, "I don't get resentments, I give 'em."

The first time I heard him say this, I had to wonder. It sounds so callous and uncaring on the surface. But after thinking on it for a time and talking to him about it as well, I concluded it is a proper attitude.

I adopted this attitude not so I could go around intentionally trying to cause people to have resentments. That is not the meaning of the saying. What the saying really means is that I am going to be myself, and if other people want to resent me, that is just fine by me. That is the "I give them" portion. I allow other people to have all the resentments they like, even if those resentments are toward me. The more important part of the saying is the first half, the "I don't get resentments" part. This means I am willing to let people be who they are. It is this willingness that frees me to be who I am as well. So, what the saying is really pointing out is my willingness to participate in life while allowing others to do the same, to do so without judging, and to do so to the best of my ability. When my ability fails me, I will find myself in the middle of an opportunity, which will allow me to practice what I have learned, and, as we all know, practice makes progress . . . not perfection.

WHEN I FINALLY DID QUIT, I PROVED

TO MYSELF JUST HOW CAPABLE I AM

OF CHANGING.

I JUST DO THE BEST I CAN

WITH WHAT I HAVE WHILE

CONTINUOUSLY REMINDING

MYSELF THAT WHAT I AM

DOING IS NORMAL.

10
PRACTICE

One of the biggest myths that I have ever heard is that "practice makes perfect." At one time I believed it, simply because people told me it was so. I believed it because I wanted it to be so. I thought perfection was possible, because I wanted to be perfect, and because of this belief, I sought perfection. I implanted the idea of being perfect so deeply in my head and in my being that even when evidence showing the impossibility of attaining perfection appeared, I ignored it until it went away. If it did not go away, I simply continued to ignore it. I believe this is referred to as denial. If I ever got close to perfecting anything, it was my denial. I practiced ignoring the truth until denial became almost second nature.

Today, I practice seeking the truth. I do this for two reasons. The most obvious reason I seek the truth is that I know it is right to do so. I want to know the truth because I believe the truth will set me free—if I can handle it and use it properly—and because I believe the truth will help me become a better person. The second, and less obvious, reason I seek the truth is to help me move away from denial, to help me learn to break a habit that I became very good at performing, and one that was ruining my life. Through searching for the truth, I soon discovered that I heard many lies yet chose to believe them. The biggest, most detrimental lie is that "practice makes perfect."

I no longer see perfection as the ultimate goal. I no longer believe I must be, or become, perfect at everything, or anything, for that matter. I see no sense in chasing after something unattainable. I find it frustrating to chase after things I know are not worthy of my effort; I have placed perfection in the category of things I have no reason to pursue.

While I do not hunt perfection anymore, I do not do sloppy work, either. Knowing that perfection is out of reach has not lessened my desire to do my best. In fact, I believe it is my "character defect" of looking for perfection, which I have not completely overcome, that drives me to always do my best, regardless of the task. Knowing that perfection is out of reach just puts it in its proper place and helps me to stay in mine.

I used to believe that when I became perfect, other people would have to submit to my will because they would see that I was always right, I always knew what to do, and I always did things properly. Call it a control issue if you like, but I just call it insane now that I know the truth. The truth is that even if I were somehow able to become perfect, people would not submit to my will. In fact, many of them might do just the opposite, despising me for my awesome ability, and perhaps deciding to permanently remove me from their lives. I would not blame them, because now I understand the truth about perfection.

I see things differently these days, and I would not give you a dime for the ability to be perfect. If I were perfect I would not be able to make mistakes, and I am beginning to enjoy making mistakes. I do not enjoy making all of them, mind you, and there are some mistakes I would take back if I could, but I see my mistakes as opportunities to learn, and I enjoy learning. I went back to college to learn, and one of the most amazing things I have learned is that attending college with a positive attitude and a desire to learn is a wonderful experience. It makes the homework fun because I am doing it to learn. Homework is no longer a chore.

I now see life as a learning experience. How could it not be? From the day we are born until the day we die, we are learning—sometimes whether we want to, or are trying to, or not. Quite often, I learn without even trying. I watch the news and learn about local, national, and international events. I open an email and learn from a friend something that is happening in his life. I help someone else in recovery and learn more about myself, the program, and life in general. Life is a series of learning opportunities. Ironically, I wonder why it took me so long to learn that. The good thing is that now I do see the truth: I believe we learn until we die.

I saw this truth in my first sponsor. He was ninety-five years old and had been living his program of recovery for nearly sixty-five years at the time of his death. He told me often of the things he learned from working with me. He told me he learned more from me than I learned from him. I thought he was nuts until I began to sponsor other people—then I saw the truth and wisdom in the statement.

My first sponsor quit school after the eighth grade. He ran his own businesses until he retired, and I know he learned some things along the way. After he retired at the age of seventy-something, he went back to school, obtained a GED, and then graduated from college. Shortly before he died, he thanked me for all the things I had helped him learn. I thanked him for the opportunity.

I thanked him because I understood the value of learning. I understood how unavoidable learning really is, and that if I become a willing participant in my learning experience, life becomes much more joy-filled, more enjoyable, and more gratifying. I believe perfection is not only unattainable, but also undesirable. If I could somehow reach perfection, I would have no need for learning and my life would essentially be over, even if my body lived on.

I can learn from books. I do it all the time. I am currently attending college, and I have no plan to stop after I get a degree—there is too much to learn. I learn from the books we use in class. I can learn from watching TV if I watch the right programs, and even if I watch the wrong programs I will still learn something. By far the best lessons I have ever learned are the ones I have learned by making mistakes. I remember those lessons. Those lessons are tattooed on my brain and branded on my mind. Even though I may ignore them by repeating a mistake, I usually know I am doing it when it happens. Sometimes doing and knowing happen simultaneously. It is that close on occasion. If I do not know beforehand, then I know when I make the mistake.

Perfection held me back for years, because I did not want to make a mistake. I used the fact that I could not do something perfectly the first time to keep me from even trying many things. Today, I want to learn, so I try. If I think I need help, I ask someone who might know and be able to help. Sometimes I just try to do something I have never tried, knowing I will either make mistakes or fail miserably. I do this because in the process I will learn, while participating in my own life.

I finally understand it is not about being right or wrong and it is not about being the greatest at something. Being the best is an awful lot of work, and eventually someone else will come along and prove they are better. Being my best is what matters. In order to be my best, I must participate; I must make mistakes and I must learn from them.

While I have learned that practice does not make perfect, I continue to practice on a continuous basis. I practice the things I want to be able to do better. I try new things to see if I might like them, but I practice the things at which I want to become proficient, experienced, or skilled.

When I practice something, I become better at it. It really is that simple. In the beginning, when there was a greater opportunity for growth, I advanced in leaps and bounds. Later, when I had attained some skills, I continued to practice in order to maintain those skills even though I might not notice much, if any, real improvement in my abilities. The most important reason to practice is because whatever I practice most is what I will become.

I can practice compassion, patience, humility, kindness, love, forgiveness, serenity, and peace, and bring these things into my life. I can also practice anger, resentment, impatience, selfishness, intolerance, and anxiety, and make them part of me. The choice is mine when it comes to what I wish to practice.

In my using days—even after I got into recovery but before I knew the potential benefits of practicing positive traits—I used to thrive on anger, resentment, impatience, intolerance, and selfishness. Practicing these things gave me a feeling of control and power. When I was angry, I felt powerful, and this gave me the illusion of being able to control others through manipulation and intimidation. Impatience and intolerance helped me to put other people down, which made me feel like I was better than they were—or so I thought. Selfishness helped me feel as though I would always get what I needed because I was looking out for my own best interests. Most of the time, I practiced these things out of habit, without thinking about what I was doing.

Today I make conscious decisions about what I will practice. This process began when I discovered I had to change at least some of the things I practiced in order to recover. First, I had to quit using—anything. After I did that, and practiced the first step by acknowledging my powerlessness over my addiction, there were still eleven of the twelve steps yet to go. I learned that my using was only a symptom of my underlying issues and troubles. Hence, problems became my opportunities for growth. At first, I did not like the idea of changing my behavior. I discovered I had to change at least some things in order to stay in recovery, so I began looking at ways to rid myself of some of my most self-destructive patterns of behavior. My sponsor made suggestions, I heard things in meetings, I read books, and I listened to tapes of "open talks" to learn what others had done to change their lives. Time and time again, I heard how people were enjoying their new practices and their new habits. I heard and read how peace and serenity led to not only a happier existence, but also to having more ability to regulate oneself and one's own behavior. This led me to investigate exactly how these benefits, claimed by others, might be helpful to me in my recovery.

One of the biggest, most beneficial things I did was to stop working the program. In fact, I stopped working at recovery.

In the beginning days of my recovery, I worked the program. I worked it diligently. I did this because others told me I would reap great rewards. In the beginning, I was not loaded, and that was reward enough. I was willing to work just for recovery, because in recovery I was finding some happiness. My trouble began when I discovered how much work I was doing. To me, work has always been a "four-letter word." I have never liked to work very hard; it's been something to get through, finish, and survive. Maybe that's because, deep down, I was lazy! Why I felt the way I did about work did not seem to matter to me. I simply had to find a way around all the work. Simple recovery suddenly did not seem to be worth all the work I was asked to do. I had to find more, and I had to find a way to do it with less work. That is when I discovered practice.

Since I had always looked at work as something from which to get away, I had always resented having to work at my job—eight hours a day, five days a week, fifty weeks a year. Of course, that is not counting lunch, breaks, vacations, and sick days. When I boiled it down, I was working about 1,840 hours a year at my job out of a possible total of 8,760 hours. On top of all this, I was told I had to work the program all the time. I believed I could not do that. Then I found an easier, softer way.

I found it in the twelfth step, which discusses practicing principles in all my affairs. (I'm talking here about honesty, hopefulness, faith, courage, integrity, willingness, humility, love, discipline, patience, perseverance, awareness, and service. This list is not comprehensive, of course.) The concept of practicing principles learned in the program by applying them in real life is yet another gift of my recovery.

More importantly, I found a way around my laziness. Instead of working the program, I could practice it. Practice makes progress; I've often heard others in my program say, "We claim spiritual progress, rather than spiritual perfection." Adopting this new way of thinking might just work if I tried. What did I have to lose?

I decided I would take a shot at practicing the program. I figured I could do that far more consistently than I could work it, because I enjoy practicing things. I always enjoyed baseball practice when I was a kid, and football practice was fun, even though I did not play much during games. Practice made sense. When I practice, I allow myself to make mistakes.

I allowed myself to believe that I could do *some* work. I enjoy working with others to help them achieve recovery. I enjoy working on the help line. I even enjoy volunteering outside of my program. I decided I was not going to work the program. I discovered there is never a mention of "working the program," yet the promises "will always materialize if we work for them." I do not mind working for the promises, because I find it easier to practice the program while I allow the promises to come true.

When I heard, "The bottom line to the Twelve Steps is the bottom line in the twelfth step: Practice these principles in all our affairs," in a meeting, I fell for it completely, and began practicing.

So, I began to practice the principles; I made mistakes, but I was practicing, and mistakes were acceptable. The more I practiced, the better I became, and the fewer mistakes I made. I made fewer big mistakes—the ones that cause irreparable damage to myself or to others. I liked that a lot. I decided that when I wanted to try something new, I could practice it for a while and see how it worked for me. If I liked the results, I could stick with it; if I did not like the results, I could discard or modify the practice.

"Practice, practice, practice" became my new mantra. I discovered that what I am really doing is practicing life.

Today I am practicing life because I want to become better at living. I have heard people say they want to die clean and sober, but I want to learn to live clean and sober first. I practice today what I want to be better at tomorrow, and living is way up on the list.

I have heard, "Life is not a dress rehearsal"; however, I should know a thing or two about rehearsal. Even if life is not a dress rehearsal, today is a dress rehearsal for tomorrow.

I took ballet when I was young, for seven whole years. Before performances we practiced in a studio every week, and the night before the show, we always had a dress rehearsal. We ran through the program—we did so more than once—from beginning to end. It was still just practice, but it was on the actual stage, with the actual lights, with the big sound system and the props, in front of an actual audience consisting of our parents and only a fraction of the audience who would see the finished show. We did this because all the ingredients were necessary to make the performance feel real.

When I live my life today, I have all the things that make life real. For the most part, the things in my life today will be here tomorrow. This is not a video game where I can go back to my last save if I do not like the outcome. I know my life is not a dress rehearsal, but I am living in the same environment today that I will most likely be living in tomorrow. Therefore, I treat my today as my practice for tomorrow—on the stage, with the lights, in front of a live audience.

During dress rehearsals for ballet, we always did our best. We did not slack off; we did not resort to half measures; we gave a full-out, head-on, top-of-our-game performance, in order to be ready for the show tomorrow.

Today, I do the same thing with life and recovery. I practice today for what I know is coming tomorrow. While life can be very uncertain, throwing me many a curve ball, I know today that I have a day of recovery coming tomorrow if I want it and if I practice it today. Not only that, but I can practice all the other things I want to have tomorrow, like happiness, peace, and serenity—the good stuff. I can bring them into my life tomorrow through practicing them today, living them at this moment on the stage of life.

I have learned to practice becoming or being normal just as I practice everything else in which I desire to become proficient. I see no sense in not practicing becoming normal. Time marches on, and I am practicing anyway. Why shouldn't I practice becoming normal?

The way I practice normal is also simple. I just do the best I can with what I have while continuously reminding myself that what I am doing is normal. After all, everything I do is pretty normal these days. So is not using. For some reason, that one took a little getting used to, but it is true. For me, not using is now normal; using is abnormal. Allowing others to enjoy the things they enjoy in moderation without envying them has become normal too, although it took a little work. Yes, it took work—then it took practice.

Something I have to remember is that this stuff is not always easy, and it does not happen overnight. Even when I find I have made considerable progress and notice I have something down pat, I will occasionally fall back into my old thinking. This is normal for me, and I must remind myself of this fact. I must allow for mistakes. Mistakes are normal.

There is only one mistake I must not allow, and that mistake is picking up. That is not normal, at least not for me, not anymore. Because using is not normal—actually, it is deadly for me—I must avoid it if I want to consider myself normal.

In fact, as I have grown to know myself, I have discovered that I can actually consider myself quite normal. In fact, I'm every bit as normal as some people, and more normal than others. Oh, sure, there are many people who are "more normal" than I am—so I guess that just puts me in the middle somewhere—and these days, that's just where I want to be!